QUANTITATIVE METHODS

The Business Briefings series consists of short and authoritative introductory textbooks in core business topics. Written by leading academics, they take a no-nonsense, practical approach and provide students with a clear and succinct overview of the subject.

These textbooks put the needs of students first, presenting the topics in a meaningful way that will help students to gain an understanding of the subject area. Covering the basics and providing springboards to further study, these books are ideal as accessible introductions or as revision guides.

Other books in the Business Briefings series:

Research Methods, by Peter Stokes

Marketing, by Jonathan Groucutt

Organizational Behaviour, by Mike Maughan

Human Resource Management, by Michael Nieto

Financial Accounting, by Jill Collis

Management Accounting, by Jill Collis

QUANTITATIVE METHODS

LES OAKSHOTT

TEACHING ASSOCIATE, WARWICK BUSINESS SCHOOL,
UNIVERSITY OF WARWICK, UK

palgrave
macmillan

First published 2014 by
PALGRAVE MACMILLAN

Palgrave Macmillan in the UK is an imprint of Macmillan Publishers Limited,
registered in England, company number 785998, of Houndmills, Basingstoke,
Hampshire RG21 6XS.

Palgrave Macmillan in the US is a division of St Martin's Press LLC,
175 Fifth Avenue, New York, NY 10010.

Palgrave Macmillan is the global academic imprint of the above companies
and has companies and representatives throughout the world.

Palgrave® and Macmillan® are registered trademarks in the United States,
the United Kingdom, Europe and other countries.

ISBN 978–1–137–34085–6

This book is printed on paper suitable for recycling and made from fully
managed and sustained forest sources. Logging, pulping and manufacturing
processes are expected to conform to the environmental regulations of the
country of origin.

A catalogue record for this book is available from the British Library.

A catalog record for this book is available from the Library of Congress.

Typeset by MPS Limited, Chennai, India.

Printed in China

CONTENTS

LIST OF FIGURES

LIST OF TABLES

PREFACE TO QUANTITATIVE METHODS

With the rapid rise in tuition fees, many students find the purchase of a traditional text book is something that they have to compromise on, and either rely on lecturer handouts or borrow textbooks from friends or the library. This approach unfortunately gives a rather superficial understanding of a subject – particularly quantitative methods, which many students find difficult.

The idea of the Palgrave series 'Business Briefings' is to produce a book that is succinct but that covers the basics of the subject. This means the book will be much more affordable to the average student. Students will still need to consult other texts to widen their knowledge of the subject, but it will offer a good introduction to the subject, and can be easily used for revision purposes.

Most quantitative methods courses taught at university and college will contain a mixture of statistics and quantitative techniques. This book is divided into two parts. The first part, which is the largest, contains all that is needed for a basics statistics module. The second part contains the four most popular quantitative techniques of investment appraisal, time series analysis, linear programming and critical path analysis. While most of the statistics chapters are normally tackled in sequence (except index numbers which is free standing), the quantitative techniques part can be tackled in any order.

Each chapter has the same structure, which is:

Objectives

Introduction

Case study

Main content

Key points

Further reading

Revision questions

The case studies show how quantitative methods are used to solve real and relevant problems. In many cases only a summary of the approach can be provided, as the techniques used are often more demanding than covered in this text. However, they do provide a glimpse of the power of quantitative methods in today's complex environment.

Within the main content the basics of the topic are explained and examples provided to show how the techniques are applied. Although the examples used are contrived they do present the type of problems that might be met in business today.

The Key points section is a useful summary of the chapter and will be invaluable as part of a revision strategy.

The Further reading section gives some relevant texts to further understanding of each topic.

The Revision questions are based on the material found in the chapter and should allow the reader to gauge his or her understanding of the techniques covered. Solutions to these questions can be found in the companion website (http://www.palgrave.com/companion/Oakshott-Quantitative-Methods.)

ACKNOWLEDGEMENTS

The author and publishers are grateful for permission to reproduce the following copyright material:

- Operational Research Society for permission to include details of 'Air traffic control, business regulation and CO2 emissions', 2012, OR Insight
- Operational Research Society for permission to include details of 'Predicting ambulance demand using singular spectrum analysis' 2012, Journal of the Operational Research Society
- Business Case Studies LLP for permission to use Tables 10.1 and 10.2
- NatCen Social Research for details from the British Social Attitudes Survey

1
COLLECTING DATA: SURVEYS AND SAMPLES

OBJECTIVES

- To understand the difference between a sampling frame, a sample and a population
- To understand the difference between probabilistic and non-probabilistic sampling
- To know how to select the correct sampling method in different situations
- To understand how to design a questionnaire

INTRODUCTION

Many decisions made by business and by the government are the result of information obtained from sample data, as it is often too costly or impractical to collect data for the whole population.

Data may already exist or it may need to be collected. When we have to collect our own data we call it *primary* data. When it already exists, as in government statistics, we call it *secondary* data. The collection of data can take many forms, but in this chapter we will concentrate on data that is collected by carrying out surveys. During the UK General Election in 2010 many surveys were undertaken by market research companies. The purpose of these surveys was not just to try and understand how people might vote but also to look at attitudes to issues and leaders, for example. Most of these surveys would have been conducted by telephone or face-to-face,

1

although in some other less urgent surveys people are sent questionnaires by post or email or asked to complete a questionnaire online.

In the surveys undertaken during the UK General Election a lot of care would have gone into selecting a representative sample of the target population. The samples had to be representative of the gender, age profile and ethnicity of the population being surveyed as well as other attributes that might be considered to affect people's voting intentions or views. The number of people being surveyed would also be calculated to ensure that a specified level of accuracy was obtained. A fuller discussion of accuracy issues when taking samples of data is given in Chapter 7.

As well as discussing ways of collecting samples of data this chapter also discusses questionnaire design because it is very important to ensure that the type and wording of questions is given proper attention if the analysis is to be of use.

British Social Attitudes survey

Every year NatCen Social Research (NatCen) undertakes a survey where it asks over 3000 people in Britain what it is like to live and work in the UK. It has been conducted annually since 1983 which makes it NatCen's longest running survey. Respondents are chosen at random using the Post Office Postcode address file. The survey is conducted face to face and is partly paper based and partly by computer. The 2011 survey covered such areas as health, immigration, welfare, Scottish Independence and transport. The interviewer had to complete around an hour's worth of questions and a small sample is given in Table 1.1 below. As well as the questions there are instructions for the interviewer. The sample size for each question is given on the far right of each question (all 3311), and the results of three questions are given as percentages at the end of this table.

CASE STUDY

Table 1.1 Sample questions from the 2011 British Social Attitudes survey

Q264 [SocSpnd1] * N=3311
CARD B2
Some people think that there should be more government spending
  on social security, while other people disagree. For each of
  the groups I read out please say whether you would like to
  see **more** or **less** government spending on them than now. Bear
  in mind that if you want more spending, this would probably
  mean that you would have to pay more taxes. If you want less
  spending, this would probably mean paying less taxes.
Firstly, ... READ OUT ...
benefits for unemployed people: would you like to see more or
  less government spending than now?
Q265 [SocSpnd2] *
                    N=3311
CARD B2 AGAIN
(Would you like to see more or less government spending
  than now on ...)
... benefits for disabled people who cannot work?
Q266 [SocSpnd3] *
                    N=3311
CARD B2 AGAIN
(Would you like to see more or less government spending
  than now on ...)
... benefits for parents who work on very low incomes?
Q267 [SocSpnd4] *
                    N=3311
CARD B2 AGAIN
(Would you like to see more or less government spending
  than now on ...)
... benefits for single parents?
Q268 [SocSpnd5] *
                    N=3311
CARD B2 AGAIN
(Would you like to see more or less government spending
  than now on ...)
.. benefits for retired people?
Q269 [SocSpnd6] *
                    N=3311
CARD B2 AGAIN
(Would you like to see more or less government spending
  than now on ...)
... benefits for people who care for those who are sick or
  disabled?

(continued)

Table 1.1   Continued

	SocSpnd1	SocSpnd2	SocSpnd3
	%	%	%
Spend much more	1.2	5.6	5.1
Spend more	13.8	47.1	53.2
Spend same as now	32.3	39.3	34.3
Spend less	40.9	5.0	4.5
Spend much less	9.7	0.4	0.5
Don't know	2.1	2.6	2.3
(Refusal)	0.1	0.1	0.0

Source: NatCen Social Research's British Social Attitudes survey

THE BASICS OF SAMPLING

A survey only collects information about a small subset of the *population*. The word 'population' can and often does refer to all the people in Britain or a town, but for statisticians it is also a general term used to refer to all groups or items being surveyed. For instance, it could refer to the viewing habits of all children in a town or, as you will see in a later chapter, it could refer to the weights of jars of coffee produced by a company during a week. The alternative to a survey is to question every member of the population, and when this is done it is called a *census*. Unfortunately it is expensive and very difficult to carry out a census, and also unnecessary. A survey of a small subset of the population, called a *sample*, can give surprisingly accurate results if carried out properly. This and other chapters will show you what factors must be taken into account to give accurate results.

It is crucial to be clear about the purpose of the survey as this will define your target population. Once you have selected your target population, you need to determine whether there is any list that would allow you to iden-tify every member of the population. This list is called a *sampling frame*, and examples include the electoral register, the postcode address file, a company's personnel records or even a list of all serial numbers of cars built by one car manufacturer last year. Sometimes a sampling frame is simply not available or is too difficult to obtain, in which case achieving a representative sample will be more difficult but not necessarily impossible.

Once your target population has been chosen and an appropriate sampling frame identified, it is necessary to choose your sample. If the sample is chosen badly your results will be inaccurate due to *bias* in your sample. Bias is caused by choosing a sample that is unrepresentative of the target population. To avoid bias you need to ensure that your sample is representative of the target population. You will see how this can be achieved later.

The purpose of a survey is to obtain information about a population. All other things being equal, the accuracy of the sample results will depend on the sample size; the larger the sample, the more accurate the results. A large sample will clearly cost more than a small one, although the method that is employed to collect the data will also determine the accuracy and cost of the survey. Methods of data collection range from the use of postal questionnaires to 'face-to-face' interviews. Some methods of data collection are expensive but guarantee a good response rate, while others are cheap to administer but are likely to produce quite a poor response.

Questionnaire design

Questionnaire design is more of an art than a science and there is no universal design that would be suitable for all situations. The actual design will depend on factors such as:

- The type of respondent (for example, business, consumers, children)
- The method of data collection (postal, telephone, face-to-face or online)
- The resources available

Questions are of two forms: close-ended questions and open-ended questions. Close-ended questions give the respondents a choice of answers and are generally considered much easier to answer and to analyse. However, the limited response range can give misleading results. Open-ended questions, such as 'Why did you buy this product?' allow respondents more flexibility in the type of response (you may get answers that you hadn't thought of), but of course this type of question is difficult to analyse. Close-ended questions are the most commonly used type and can take many forms, such as:

• Dichotomous questions – These are questions that have only two answers, such as 'yes' or 'no'.

• Numeric – Some questions ask for a single number, such as the distance travelled to work each day. Where the question is personal (for example, earnings or age) it is best to give a range, such as:

Less than £20 000   £20 000 to £30 000   Over £30 000

• Multiple choice – Respondents select from three or more choices (the question on salary above is an example of a multiple choice question).

• Likert scale – The question is a statement, such as 'Taxes should be increased to pay for a better health service', and respondents indicate their amount of agreement using a scale similar to the one below.

Strongly agree   Agree   Neither agree   Disagree   Strongly
nor disagree   disagree

• Semantic differential – With this type of question only two ends of the scale are provided, and the respondent selects the point between the two ends that represents his views. For example, 'The leisure facilities in my town are':

Excellent ————————————————————————— Poor

• Rank order – Respondents are asked to rank each option. This type of question is useful if you want to obtain information on relative preferences but is more difficult to analyse. The number of choices should be kept to a minimum.

Once the questionnaire has been designed you need to decide how to collect the data. Some methods require a sampling frame while others do not.

Simple random sampling

With this method every member of the target population has an equal chance of being selected. This implies that a sampling frame is required and a method of randomly selecting the required sample from this list. The simplest example of this technique is a raffle where the winning ticket is drawn from the 'hat'. For a more formal application a stream of random numbers would be used. Random numbers are numbers that show no pattern; each digit is equally likely. A table of random numbers is given in Appendix 1 or you can use the RAND function in Excel. The method of simple random sampling using random numbers is quite easy to apply, although tedious, as you will see from Example 1.1.

Example 1.1

Table 1.2 is a part of a list of students enrolled on a business studies course at a university.

Table 1.2   List of students enrolled on a business studies course

Number	Name	Gender
1	N. Adams	Male
2	C. Shah	Male
3	B. Booth	Female
4	C. Meng	Male
5	A. Ho	Male
6	D. Drew	Male
7	K. Fisher	Female
8	P. Frome	Male
9	G. Godfrey	Male
10	J. Bakoulas	Male
11	D. Jeffrey	Female
12	H. Jones	Male
13	M. Li	Male
14	N. King	Female
15	K. Lenow	Male
16	A. Loft	Female
17	T. Georgiou	Female
18	S. Moore	Female
19	F. Muper	Female
20	R. Muster	Female
21	A. Night	Male
22	J. Nott	Male
23	L. Nupper	Male
24	K. Khan	Male
25	O. Patter	Female

Say from this 'population' of 25 students you wanted to randomly select a sample of 5 students. How would you do it? You could use the student number (in this case conveniently numbered from 1 to 25) and then try and obtain a match using a stream of two-digit random numbers between 0 and 25. For example, suppose you had the following random numbers: 10, 25, 8, 23, 15, 21, 12, 19, 4, 15, 7. The first five numbers equate to J. Bakoulas, O. Patter, P. Frome, L. Nupper and K. Lenow.

One question that we should ask of any sample is how representative it is of the target population. In our population we have 15 males and 10 females which is a proportion of 60% males to 40% females. In the sample we have 4 males out of 5 which is a proportion of 80%, and on this statistic our sample doesn't represent the target population very well. Another sample might give us a completely different proportion and you could even get a sample of all the same gender. This variation is called sampling error and occurs in all sampling procedures. In Chapter 7 you will be shown how to control and quantify this error.

Stratified sampling

Many populations can be divided into different categories. For example, a population of adults consists of the two sexes, employment status, ethnicity and many other categories. If you think that the responses you will get from your survey are likely to be determined partly by each category, then clearly you want your sample to contain each category in the correct proportions.

You probably realized that the 'perfect' sample above should contain 3 males (60% of 5). In order to ensure that you will get exactly 3 males, you should first of all have separated out the two sexes and then obtained two simple random samples, one of size 3 and one of size 2, as shown in Table 1.3. The two populations have been re-numbered, although this is not essential. Using the same random numbers as before and ignoring numbers greater than 15 for the male sample and 10 for the female sample, we get male students 10, 8 and 15; that is M. Li, K. Khan and C. Shah, and female students 4 and 7, that is; D. Jeffrey and S. Moore.

Table 1.3 Table ordered by gender

Male students

Number	Name
1	N. Adams
2	J. Bakoulas
3	D. Drew
4	P. Frome
5	G. Godfrey
6	A. Ho
7	H. Jones
8	K. Khan
9	K. Lenow
10	M. Li
11	C. Meng
12	A. Night
13	J. Nott
14	L. Nupper
15	C. Shah

Female students

Number	Name
1	B. Booth
2	K. Fisher
3	T. Georgiou
4	D. Jeffrey
5	N. King
6	A. Loft
7	S. Moore
8	F. Muper
9	R. Muster
10	O. Patter

Stratified sampling is a very reliable method, but it does assume that you have a knowledge of the categories of the population. Stratified sampling is often used in conjunction with the next method.

Multi-stage sampling

If the target population covers a wide geographical area then a simple random sample may have selected respondents in quite different parts of the country. If the method employed to collect the data is of the face-to-face interview type, then clearly a great deal of travelling could be involved. To overcome this problem the area to be surveyed is divided into smaller areas and a number of these smaller areas randomly selected. If desired, the smaller areas chosen could themselves be divided into smaller districts and a random number of these selected. This procedure is continued until the area is small enough for a simple random sample (or a stratified sample) to be selected. The final sample should consist of respondents concentrated into a small number of areas. It is important that the random sample chosen from each area is the same proportion of the population or bias towards certain areas could result. As it is, bias is likely to occur as a result of similarity of responses from people within the same area, but this is the price you pay for reduced travelling time.

Example 1.2

A broadcasting company wishes to obtain a representative sample of television viewers from across Britain using multi-stage sampling.

The country could be split into counties, or perhaps television regions might be more appropriate in this case. A number of these would be chosen at random, and these areas subdivided into district councils. A random sample of districts within each chosen region could now be selected, and the selected districts divided into postal areas. A random sample of residents within each chosen postal area could then be chosen using the register of electors.

Figure 1.1 illustrates this process in diagrammatic form. At each level you are taking a random sample. Note that it is not until you get to the individual elector that you carry out the actual survey.

Cluster sampling

Cluster sampling is similar to multi-stage sampling and is used when a sampling frame is not available. Again a large geographical area is divided into a number of smaller areas called clusters. If necessary these clusters can be further subdivided to obtain clusters which are small enough for all members of the cluster to be surveyed. As with multi-stage sampling, a bias will result due to similarities in responses from members of the same cluster. The difference between cluster sampling and multi-stage sampling is that since individual members of a cluster cannot be identified in advance, it is necessary for all members to be surveyed. Random sampling is therefore not involved.

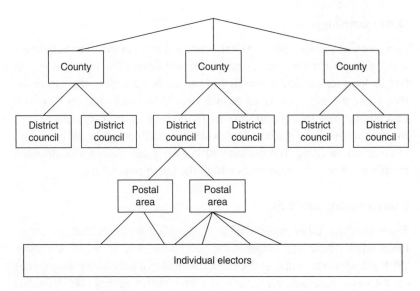

Figure 1.1 Multi-stage sampling

Systematic sampling

This method is normally used with a sampling frame, but it can also be used where a sampling frame is not available. However, in this case the size of the population must be known. The idea is that every nth member of a population is selected, where the value of n is determined by the size of the population and by the required sample size. For instance, if a 5% sample is to be selected from a population of size 1000, then every 50th person will be selected. The start of the sequence is usually chosen at random. For example, if a 20% sample was to be selected from the student population given in Table 1.2 every 5th person would be selected. If you started with, say, the third student, your sample would consist of B. Booth, P. Frome, M. Li, S. Moore and L. Nupper.

Systematic sampling is a very quick and efficient method of obtaining a sample. The sample should be random, provided there is no pattern in the way people are ordered in the population.

Quota sampling

I am sure that you have seen an interviewer in a town centre with a clipboard waiting to pounce on some unsuspecting individual! The interviewer is in fact looking for particular groups of individuals who meet the categories that he or she has been asked to interview. Within each group there will be a number or quota of people required, and the survey is complete when the quotas have been reached. Quota sampling is a non-probabilistic version of stratified sampling. The quotas within each group should, like stratified sampling, reflect the proportions within the target population.

Other sampling methods

There are three other non-probabilistic sampling methods that are sometimes used. These are judgemental, purposive and snowball sampling. With judgemental sampling the researcher makes a judgement about what constitutes a representative sample. If a government agency was interested in the effects on people's health of car exhaust fumes, they would choose areas near cities or motorways to obtain the sample. They would not choose rural areas, except perhaps for a control group. Purposive sampling is where certain members of the population are purposefully chosen. For example, customers holding store loyalty cards might be asked about planned improvements to the store. Snowballing is where a sample is chosen using one of the methods mentioned in this chapter and then additional members of the population are generated from this sample. An example could be in the investigation of the mis-selling of pensions that occurred in Britain during the late 1980s. A sample of pensioners could be obtained and any person who was persuaded to leave their occupational pension scheme would be asked to name other people they knew who were also affected. In this way the sample size could be increased.

KEY POINTS

It is generally impractical to question or observe every member of the target population, so a sample of this population is selected instead.

Table 1.4 A summary of the sampling methods available

	Sampling frame available (probabilistic sampling)	Sampling frame not available (non-probabilistic sampling)
Population resides in one place	Simple random sampling Systematic sampling	Systematic sampling (if the size of the population is known) Judgemental sampling Purposive sampling
Population geographically scattered	Multi-stage sampling	Cluster sampling Judgemental sampling
Population is defined by categories	Stratified sampling	Quota sampling
Population is small and unknown		Snowballing

To obtain data from a population of people you normally carry out a survey. This survey can be done by post, by telephone, face-to-face and online. Each method has its advantages and disadvantages. A face-to-face survey normally gives you the best response rate but is more costly than other methods.

Whatever method you use the sample should be representative of the target population.

★ Probabilistic sampling methods will give you a representative sample but require a sampling frame.
★ Non-probabilistic sampling is generally quicker to carry out but may not be completely representative of the target population.

Table 1.4 summarizes the different sampling methods available.

FURTHER READING

There are a huge number of quantitative methods and statistical texts that cover the collection of data. Some like Morris (2008), Curwin and Slater (2008) and Chapter 3 in Oakshott (2012) cover similar material to this text. Collis and Hussey (2009) is a more general text on business research methods. Fowler (2009) is a very detailed text on survey research methods and would be ideal for anyone having to design their own survey.

REVISION QUESTIONS

1 A town with historical connections has received a grant of £20m in order to improve its tourist facilities. The town councillors have decided to ask a representative sample of residents how the money should be spent. Given that expenditure for the survey must be kept to a minimum suggests ways in which a representative sample of residents can be chosen.

2 Which of the following are likely to have a sampling frame?
- Students at a university
- Employees of a company
- Concert goers
- Shoppers at a shopping mall
- Members of a social networking group

3 A company wishes to carry out a survey of its employees to monitor their views on the future of the company. A departmental breakdown of the company's 200 employees is as follows:

Shop-floor/warehouse	80
Service engineers	15
Quality control	20
Marketing and sales	25
Accounts	15
Personnel	10
Administration	25
Catering	10

A survey of 40 employees is to be conducted. A sampling frame is available, listing the employees by surname in alphabetical order, independent of department.

(a) Explain how the following sampling methods could be carried out to obtain the sample of 40 employees:
- simple random sampling
- systematic sampling
- stratified sampling
- quota sampling

(b) Discuss the benefits and drawbacks of using quota sampling to obtain the sample of 40 employees.

4 You have been asked to conduct a survey into the attitudes of school leavers to higher education. You intend to carry this out using the face-to-face interview method. How would you obtain your sample?

2

DESCRIBING DATA USING TABLES AND CHARTS

OBJECTIVES

- To be able to distinguish between different types of data
- To be able to tabulate data into an ungrouped or a grouped frequency table, as appropriate
- To be able to use diagrams to present data, and to know how to draw appropriate conclusions from these diagrams

INTRODUCTION

The human brain finds it difficult to make sense of a large quantity of data. However, when data is organized and presented in a diagrammatic form, we find it much easier to pick out patterns. This is the opposite to computers which can easily process vast quantities of data but find pattern recognition extremely difficult. This chapter first discusses the type of data that you may come across, and then looks at the best ways of displaying it.

2011 UK Census

A national census is undertaken every 10 years. The purpose of the census is to take a snapshot of the population of the UK and to obtain statistics on a whole range of demographic information, including age and ethnic profile, employment, car ownership and health. From this information the government can decide how and where to allocate resources such as new schools, roads and hospitals. One question asked household residents how healthy they felt; using a five-point scale from very good health to very bad health. The results can be shown in a simple bar chart (Figure 2.1) where it can be seen that the vast majority of people considered themselves to be in very good or good health.

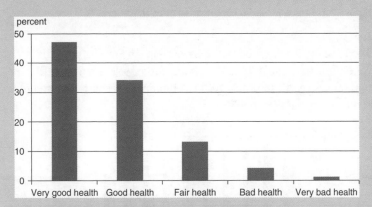

Figure 2.1 Census result on general health of residents

Source: Office for National Statistics, 2011 Census data from KS301EW, not directly comparable with 2001 census due to a response option change

Another question concerned the highest-level qualifications residents had. The results are shown in the pie chart (Figure 2.2). This chart clearly shows that most people (27%) have level 4 qualifications and above (higher education), followed by people with no qualifications (23%).

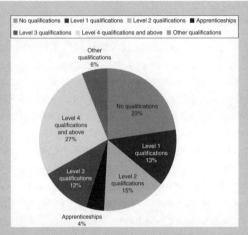

Figure 2.2 Census result on highest level of qualification

Source: Census – Office for National Statistics

There was also a question on car ownership. The results this time were compared across the different regions as well as between the two census years (2001 and 2011). A multiple bar chart was used to compare the data (Figure 2.3).

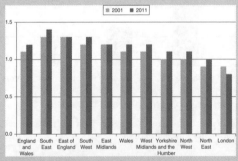

Figure 2.3 Census result on the question of car ownership

Source: Office for National Statistics, 2011 Census data from KS17, 2011 Census data from KS404EW

This diagram shows that in all areas except London car ownership has increased in the 10 years between the two censuses.

DATA CLASSIFICATION

To classify data we need to define how it is measured. These are four *levels of measurement*. These are:

1. Continuous data – Data that is measured on a scale, such as weight or temperature. Continuous data can be further subdivided into interval-scale data and ratio-scale data. An interval scale has no true starting (zero) point, so although it is possible to comment on the interval between measurements, it is not possible to compare the ratio of one to the other. For example, temperature (in Celsius and Fahrenheit) is measured on an interval-scale: you can say that 24C is twelve degrees hotter than 12C, but you cannot say that 24C is twice as hot as 12C. Ratio-scaled data, on the other hand, can be compared on a ratio basis as well as on an interval basis. For example, weight is measured on a ratio scale; 24 kg is twice as much as 12 kg, as well as being 12 kg different.

2. Discrete data – Data that takes on whole values. The obvious example of discrete data is data obtained by counting, such as the number of defective items in a batch. An important aspect of discrete data is that it cannot be subdivided (for example, you can't have half a defective item).

3. Ordinal data – Data that can be arranged in some meaningful order. An example of this type of data is the assessment consumers might give to a product. They might be asked to rate the product using a score from 1 to 5, where 5 is 'excellent' and 1 is 'poor'. Although 5 is better than 1, it is not necessarily 5 times better or even 4 points better.

4. Nominal data – Data that does not have a numerical value and can only be placed in a suitable category. An example of this is hair colour or choice of newspaper. All we can do with nominal data is to separate it into its categories.

Ordinal and nominal data are usually referred to as *categorical* data.

To summarize:

- *Ratio data* – Statistically the highest level of data. It has a defined zero so that data can be compared by interval and ratio.
- *Interval* – There is no defined zero, so we can only compare intervals.
- *Discrete* – It is meaningful to give data only in whole numbers. Discrete data is usually obtained by counting.
- *Ordinal* – Ordinal data has order, but the interval between measurements is not meaningful.
- *Nominal* – Nominal data has no order, and little statistical analysis can be done with this data.

The further you go down the hierarchy, the less the statistical analysis that can be carried out on the data. An important point to note, though, is that data can be manipulated downwards but not upwards. For example, data on ages could be placed into groups, such as: group 1, less than 20; group 2, from 20 to 30, etc. This could then be treated as ordinal data. It is of course not possible to give nominal data (such as mode of travel) a number and then to treat the numbers as ordinal data.

TABULATION OF DATA

Example 2.1

A small survey was carried out into the mode of travel to work. The information in Table 2.1 relates to a random sample of 20 employed adults.

This is categorical (nominal) data since mode of travel does not have a numerical value. This information would be better displayed as a frequency table (Table 2.2).

Frequency is simply the number of times each category appeared. As well as the actual frequency, the *relative frequency* has been calculated. This is

Table 2.1 Data for Example 2.1

Person	Mode of travel	Person	Mode of travel
1	Car	11	Car
2	Car	12	Bus
3	Bus	13	Walk
4	Car	14	Car
5	Walk	15	Train
6	Cycle	16	Bus
7	Car	17	Car
8	Cycle	18	Cycle
9	Bus	19	Car
10	Train	20	Car

Table 2.2 Frequency table

Mode of travel	Frequency	Relative frequency (%)
Car	9	45
Bus	4	20
Cycle	3	15
Walk	2	10
Train	2	10
Total	20	

the frequency expressed as a percentage and is calculated by dividing a frequency by the total frequency and multiplying by 100.

Example 2.2

The data in Table 2.3 gives the number of foreign holidays sold by a travel agent over the past four weeks.

This is discrete data as it would have been obtained by counting. By examining the figures you should see that 10 sales occur most frequently, although

Table 2.3 Frequency table for Example 2.2

Day	No. Sold	Day	No. Sold
Monday	10	Monday	13
Tuesday	12	Tuesday	10
Wednesday	9	Wednesday	12
Thursday	10	Thursday	8
Friday	22	Friday	12
Saturday	14	Saturday	12
Monday	11	Monday	11
Tuesday	18	Tuesday	13
Wednesday	10	Wednesday	10
Thursday	10	Thursday	14
Friday	11	Friday	13
Saturday	9	Saturday	12

Table 2.4 Ungrouped frequency table for Example 2.2

Number Sold	Frequency
8	1
9	2
10	6
11	3
12	5
13	3
14	2
More than 14	2

there is a range from 8 to 22 sales. To enable this information to be seen more clearly you could aggregate the data into a table (Table 2.4).

This table is called an *ungrouped frequency table*, since the numbers sold have not been grouped. This table is a useful way of summarizing a small set of discrete data. There are two extreme values or *outliers* of value 18 and

22 sales and these have been included by the use of a 'more than' quantity. From this table you can see that between 10 and 12 holidays are usually sold each day.

Example 2.3

Table 2.5 gives the number of bolts produced by a machine each hour over the past 65 hours, while Table 2.6 gives the length in mm of 80 of these bolts.

It is not easy to see any patterns in the data without some kind of grouping.

An ungrouped frequency table for either set of data would not be very helpful for two reasons: for both data sets the range of the data is large,

Table 2.5 Hourly rate of bolt production

184	250	136	178	231	158	197	159	141	218
223	156	124	177	298	175	231	218	117	149
169	119	174	171	191	202	214	138	127	254
177	181	189	201	198	165	140	100	147	188
296	237	223	267	147	112	238	139	165	125
165	188	230	150	127	251	182	139	159	179
230	183	166	163	194					

Table 2.6 Length of bolts (mm)

49.9	53.8	61.3	45.8	51.2	44.5	55.3	51.4	84.1
55.7	52.7	68.7	52.5	58.8	37.8	44.1	49.9	43.8
64.1	35.9	46.4	45.1	30.6	45.9	54.8	54.0	49.3
46.8	46.5	52.2	33.3	42.9	47.7	46.2	40.5	36.8
47.5	46.3	70.2	35.5	56.7	56.0	56.5	49.5	57.5
52.0	36.8	46.3	42.4	30.2	49.5	36.3	44.6	45.1
30.0	47.0	52.1	53.0	46.1	50.5	56.0	50.9	42.7
42.1	51.2	49.0	49.9	54.4	53.2	43.0	41.3	49.7
42.9	61.1	41.7	35.7	45.0	59.2	60.6	44.7	

which would necessitate a large table, and for Table 2.6 the data is continuous. Continuous data can, by definition, take on any value, so what values would we use in a table? To overcome these problems a *grouped frequency table* is produced. A grouped frequency table is similar to an ungrouped table except that intervals are defined into which the data can be grouped. The number and size of each interval depends on the quantity and range of your data. In general you would have between 8 and 15 intervals and the width of each interval, or the class interval, should be a convenient number such as 10, 20, 25, etc. In the case of Table 2.5 the range is 298 − 100 = 198, and a class interval of 20 would give you 10 intervals, which is about right. The first interval would be 100 to 119, the second 120 to 139, and so on. Once you have decided on the size of each interval you need to allocate each value to one of the intervals. This can be done by using a tally chart. This has been done in Table 2.7.

The next stage is to add up the tally in each interval to give you the frequency. The final grouped frequency table is as shown in Table 2.8. From this table it appears that the rate of production is quite variable, although the rate is unlikely to be less than 120 or more than 240 bolts per hour.

Table 2.7 Tally chart

Class interval	Tally
100 to 119	||||
120 to 139	ⅣⅡ |||
140 to 159	ⅣⅡ ⅣⅡ
160 to 179	ⅣⅡ ⅣⅡ |||
180 to 199	ⅣⅡ ⅣⅡ |
200 to 219	ⅣⅡ
220 to 239	ⅣⅡ |||
240 to 259	|||
260 to 279	|
280 to 299	||

Table 2.8 Grouped frequency table

Interval	Frequency	Relative frequency (%)
100 to 119	4	6.2
120 to 139	8	12.3
140 to 159	10	15.4
160 to 179	13	20.0
180 to 199	11	16.9
200 to 219	5	7.7
220 to 239	8	12.3
240 to 259	3	4.6
260 to 279	1	1.5
280 to 299	2	3.1
Total	65	100

To group the data in Table 2.6 you need to decide on a suitable interval. You might decide on a class interval of 5 mm, which would give you 11 intervals. Since the smallest length is 30 mm the first group would start at 30 mm, the second at 35 mm, and so on. But what should the end of each group be? If you used 34 mm you would not be able to allocate a value between 34 and 35 mm. You cannot use the same figure for both the end of one group and the start of the next because this would allow a value to be added to more than one group. It is essential that a value can go into one, and only one, interval, so the ranges must be designed to guarantee this. Since the data is continuous the length can be quoted to any degree of accuracy, so the end of each group would be defined as under 35 mm and under 40 mm, and so on. In this way a length of 34.9 mm would be in the first group while 35.0 mm would be in the second group.

If we use this grouping we would get Table 2.9.

This table gives a clearer *distribution* of the data and we see that 77.5% of the values are between 40 mm and 60 mm, with few over 60 mm or less than 40 mm.

Table 2.9 Grouped frequency table for the length of bolts

Interval	Frequency	Relative frequency (%)
30 to under 35 mm	4	5.00
35 to under 40 mm	7	8.75
40 to under 45 mm	14	17.50
45 to under 50 mm	23	28.75
50 to under 55 mm	16	20.00
55 to under 60 mm	9	11.25
60 to under 65 mm	4	5.00
65 to under 70 mm	1	1.25
70 to under 75 mm	1	1.25
75 to under 80 mm	0	0
80 to under 85 mm	1	1.25

For the data in Example 2.3 the class intervals were the same for the whole distribution, that is, 20 in the first case and 5 in the second. However, it is not necessary for the intervals to be equal and you may have two or more different intervals in the same table. In Table 2.9 you might decide to condense the last four intervals into one since the frequencies in these intervals are small. If you do this your last interval will be 65 to under 85 mm, which has a frequency of 2. It is also possible to have an open interval at the beginning or end, such as greater than 70 mm or less than 30 mm. However, only use open intervals if you really have to and only if there is a relatively small number of items in this interval.

DIAGRAMMATIC REPRESENTATION OF DATA

Although frequency tables can give you more information than the raw data, it can still be difficult to take in all the information that is inherent in the data. Diagrams can help provide this additional information and also display the data in a more visually attractive manner. You do lose some detail, but this is a small price to pay for the additional information that diagrams provide. There are several types of diagram and the choice depends mainly on the type of data, but also on your intended audience. The Statistical Bulletin provided by the Office for National Statistics used simple diagrams to represent the results from the 2011 census and some of these diagrams were presented in the case study at the start of this chapter.

These days most people will use a spreadsheet when producing diagrams. Spreadsheets can produce high-quality charts which can be easily updated if the data changes. However, some experience of drawing diagrams by hand is still useful.

Example 2.4

The sales by department of a high street store over the past three years are shown in Table 2.10.

An inspection of the data in Table 2.10 reveals that the total sales have increased over the three years, although clothing has shown a decline. Diagrams should help bring out these and other differences more clearly.

Pie charts

When you want to compare the relative sizes of the frequencies a pie chart is a good choice of diagram. It is normally used for categorical data, and each category is represented by a segment of a circle. The size of each segment reflects the frequency of that category and can be represented as an angle. It is rare for people to draw a pie chart by hand as a protractor is required to measure the angles, but if you need to, the angle is calculated by working out the percentage of the category and then multiplying by

Table 2.10 Sales by department and year

	2009	2010	2011
Clothing	£1.7m	£1.4m	£1.4m
Furniture	£3.4m	£4.9m	£5.6m
Electrical goods	£0.2m	£0.4m	£0.5m
Total	£5.3m	£6.7m	£7.5m

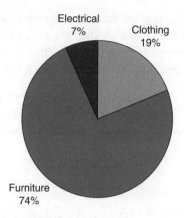

Figure 2.4 Pie chart for sales in 2011

360. For example, for the sales for 2011 in Example 2.4 the angle would be calculated as follows:

Clothing as a percentage is $\dfrac{1.4}{7.5} \times 100 = 18.7\%$

The angle is therefore $\dfrac{18.7}{100} \times 360 = 67°$

The complete pie chart for the sales for 2011 is shown in Figure 2.4. This diagram demonstrates that the furniture department has contributed the bulk of the total sales for this year.

Bar charts

Although pie charts tend to be a popular means of comparing the size of categories they have the disadvantage that they are not suitable for displaying several sets of data simultaneously. You would, for instance, need three separate pie charts to represent the data in Table 2.10. A *simple bar chart* is another useful method of displaying categorical data, or an ungrouped frequency table. For each category a vertical bar is drawn, the height of the

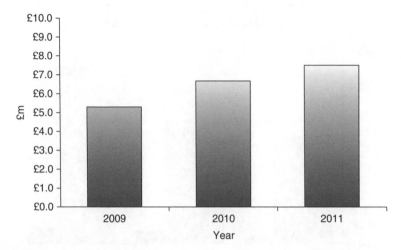

Figure 2.5 A simple bar chart of total sales

bar being proportional to the frequency. The diagram in Figure 2.5 shows the total sales in the form of a simple bar chart.

When a category is subdivided into several subcategories the simple bar chart is not really adequate as you would need a different bar chart for each subcategory. A *multiple bar chart* is used when you are interested in changes in the components, but the totals are of no interest. Figure 2.6 is a multiple bar chart for the data in Table 2.10.

If you are interested in comparing totals and seeing how the totals are made up a *component* bar chart is used. Figure 2.7 is a component bar chart for the data in Table 2.10. In this figure you can see the variation in total sales from year to year, as well as seeing how each department contributes to total sales. If you are more interested in the proportion of sales in each department a *percentage* bar chart may be of more interest. This is shown in Figure 2.8. This chart is rather like the pie chart but has the advantage that several sets of data can be displayed simultaneously.

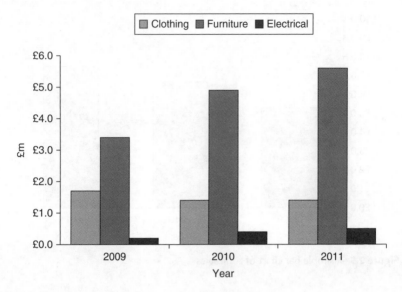

Figure 2.6 A multiple bar chart

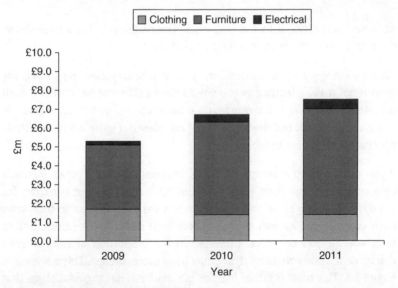

Figure 2.7 A component bar chart

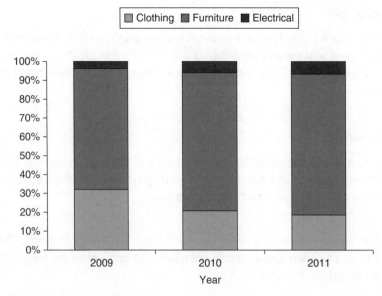

Figure 2.8 A percentage bar chart

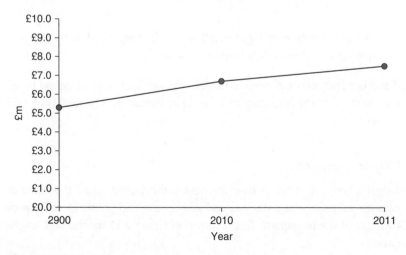

Figure 2.9 Line graph

Line graphs

When data is in the form of a time series a line graph can be a useful means of showing any trends in the data. Figure 2.9 is a line graph for the total sales given in Table 2.10 and clearly shows the rise in sales over the three years.

Histograms

For grouped frequency tables a different type of diagram is normally used. This diagram is called a *histogram* and although it may look like a bar chart there are some important differences. These are:

- The horizontal axis is a continuous scale, just like a normal graph. This implies that there should not be gaps between bars unless the frequency for that class interval really is zero.

- It is the area of the bars that is being compared, not the heights. This means that if one class interval is twice the others then the height must be halved, since area = width × height.

The histogram shown in Figure 2.10 is for the lengths of bolts given in Example 2.3 and uses an equal class interval of 5 mm.

If the last four intervals were combined, the last class interval would be 20 mm. In this case the frequency of 3 should be divided by 4 (since 20 is 4 × 5) to give 0.75.

Frequency polygons

To get a better idea about how the data is distributed across the range of possible values of the data, you can join up the mid points of the top of each bar of the histogram. This is shown in Figure 2.11 for the bolt length data.

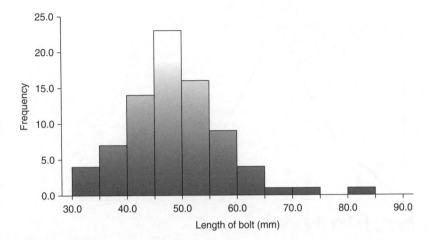

Figure 2.10 Histogram of length of bolt

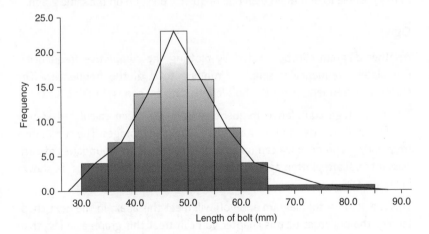

Figure 2.11 Histogram with mid points joined up

If the bars are now removed, you are left with a picture of the shape of the underlying distribution of the data. The area under the frequency polygon is the same as the area under the original histogram (Figure 2.12).

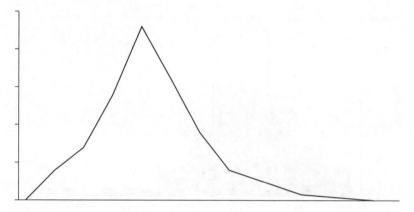

Figure 2.12 Frequency polygon

This diagram can be quite useful if you want to compare different distributions, as it is possible to plot more than one frequency polygon on the same graph.

Ogive

Another diagram can be created by plotting the *cumulative* frequencies. Cumulative frequency is simply a running total of the frequencies. The cumulative frequencies for the bolt length data are shown in Table 2.11.

The percentage cumulative frequencies have also been calculated as you will find that the use of percentages has certain advantages. The cumulative frequency graph or *ogive* can now be drawn. The *upper* boundaries of each class interval are plotted against the (%) cumulative frequencies, as shown in Figure 2.13.

This is a very useful diagram and you will meet this again in the next chapter. For the purposes of this chapter you can treat this graph as a less than graph, since the upper-class boundaries were plotted against the cumulative frequencies. So, for example, 13.75% of the lengths are below 40 mm.

Stem and leaf plot

This can be a useful diagram particularly when there is little data. In this plot the most significant digit is the *stem* and the least significant digit is

Table 2.11 Calculation of cumulative frequencies

Interval	Frequency	Cumulative frequency	% Cumulative frequency
30 to under 35 mm	4	4	5.00
35 to under 40 mm	7	11	13.75
40 to under 45 mm	14	25	31.25
45 to under 50 mm	23	48	60.00
50 to under 55 mm	16	64	80.00
55 to under 60 mm	9	73	91.25
60 to under 65 mm	4	77	96.25
65 to under 70 mm	1	78	97.50
70 to under 75 mm	1	79	98.75
75 to under 80 mm	0	79	98.75
80 to under 85 mm	1	80	100.00

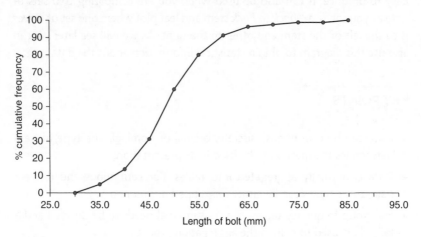

Figure 2.13 Ogive

the *leaf*. So in the length of bolt data where the data varies between 30 mm and 80 mm, the stem would be represented by the tens unit (3 to 8) and the leaf by the remaining digit (the decimal value would be ignored). As stem values 3 to 8 only gives 6 levels it is useful to split the stem into 2 as you can see in Table 2.12.

Table 2.12 A stem and leaf plot of the length of bolt data

```
Frequency     Stem &   Leaf
     4.00        3 .  | 0003
     7.00        3 .  | 5556667
    14.00        4 .  | 01122222334444
    23.00        4 .  | 55555666666677799999999
    16.00        5 .  | 0011122222333444
     9.00        5 .  | 556666789
     4.00        6 .  | 0114
     3.00  Extremes   | (>=68)

                  3|3 represents 33 mm
```

The 3 values above 65 mm can be represented as *outliers* as shown. This diagram clearly shows the shape of the distribution and can be quick and easy to produce. It can also be used when you are comparing two sets of data as you can use *a back to back* stem and leaf plot where one set of leaves is to the left of the stem and other to the right. As we will see later we can also use this diagram to obtain statistical information about the data.

KEY POINTS

★ Data can be continuous, discrete, ordinal or nominal. The type of data determines the method to be used in its presentation.

★ Data is normally aggregated into tables. For continuous and discrete data, these tables can be either ungrouped or grouped.

★ For group frequency tables, the class interval needs to be decided and a tally chart used to help in the aggregation process.

★ Several different types of diagram can be used to display the data more effectively.

★ Pie charts can only be used for categorical data.

★ Bar charts are normally used for categorical data and for discrete data. There are 3 main types of bar charts: these are the simple bar chart, component bar chart and the multiple bar chart.

★ Line graphs can be used for time series data.

★ Histograms are used either for continuous or for discrete data that has been aggregated into a frequency table. A histogram gives you an idea of the shape of the underlying distribution, but a frequency polygon will show this more clearly.

★ If cumulative frequencies are plotted, a cumulative frequency ogive is obtained. This important graph allows you to obtain further information about the underlying distribution.

★ Another useful diagram is a stem and leaf plot. This diagram allows the shape of the distribution to be seen and outliers can be highlighted.

FURTHER READING

All elementary statistics books will contain a chapter on representing data using tables and charts. Chapter 4 of Oakshott (2012) also contains details using Excel and SPSS to produce professional looking charts.

REVISION QUESTIONS

1 How would you define the following sets of data?
   (a) Measurement of the weights of jars of coffee
   (b) Choice of summer holiday
   (c) Weekly earnings by employees at a factory
   (d) Numbers of students following a business studies course
   (e) Market research survey into consumer reaction to a new product

2 Using the data in Example 2.4 and Figures 2.3 to 2.7 summarize in words how sales have varied by department and year.

3 Using the example on lengths of bolts (Example 2.3) determines the proportion of lengths that are:
   (a) below 50 mm
   (b) below 41 mm
   (c) above 63 mm

4 Table 2.13 is taken from the 2001 national census. It shows the highest qualification held by men and women.

(a) Draw a suitable bar chart to compare the qualifications of male and female residents.

(b) Draw a pie chart of the total figures and compare it with the results from the 2011 census (see the case study at the start of this chapter).

Table 2.13 Level of highest qualifications (aged 16–74), England, Wales and Northern Ireland by gender

	Gender		
	Male	Female	Total
No. qualifications	165	187	352
Level 1	99	99	198
Level 2	107	124	231
Level 3	48	50	98
Level 4/5	117	117	234
Other qualifications/level unknown (England Wales only)	51	28	79
Total	587	605	1192

5 The data below relates to the weight (in grams) of an item produced by a machine.

```
28.8   29.2   30.8   29.2   30.2   30.0   26.8   30.6   29.0   27.8
28.6   30.4   30.8   29.2   30.4   29.6   31.4   30.6   31.0   31.4
31.4   30.0   29.0   29.4   29.0   28.0   26.5   29.6   27.0   23.2
25.2   24.5   28.0   27.0   29.4   27.6   26.2   25.3   26.8   25.8
28.2   28.1   30.0   30.0   27.1   26.1   25.4   23.8   22.8   23.5
25.5   24.0   27.0   28.5   27.2   25.5   25.6   24.5   23.5   22.4
25.2   27.4   27.0   28.2   28.0   28.0   25.8   30.4   26.5   25.2
29.3   27.4   22.1   26.2   23.8   24.8   20.5   20.4   24.6   24.8
```

(a) Aggregate this data into a suitable frequency table.

(b) Draw a histogram of the data.

(c) Draw a stem and leaf plot of the data.

(d) Draw a cumulative frequency ogive of the data and demonstrate how it could be used to provide further information about the distribution of weights.

(e) What conclusions can be made about the data from your diagrams?

3

DESCRIBING DATA USING SIMPLE STATISTICS

OBJECTIVES

- To be able to calculate measures of central tendency (measures of location) and variation in the data (spread around the central location)
- To understand the advantages and disadvantages of different measures
- To be able to draw suitable charts to help calculate some of these measures

INTRODUCTION

Although tables and diagrams allow important features of data to be displayed, these methods of summarizing information are generally qualitative rather than quantitative. In order to provide more quantitative information, it is necessary to calculate statistical measures that can be used to represent the entire set of data. Two important measures of the data are the location of the data, in terms of a typical or central value, and the spread or dispersion of the data around this central value.

Average Length of Stay in A&E

Government guidelines (2010) stated that 95% of patients should have a maximum length of stay in A&E of 4 hours. During 2010–2011 there were 16 million admissions to A&E departments in England, and 94.2% of patients were treated with this 4 hour target. The average (mean) attendance time in the A&E department, from arrival to departure, was 146 minutes (2 hrs 26 min). Of course average length of stay will vary depending on time of day. Table 3.1 shows average length of stay in A&E in England during 2010–2011 by arrival time.

Table 3.1 Average length of stay in A&E during 2010–2011

Hour (arrival)	Mean (average) duration to departure
00:00	226
01:00	177
02:00	176
03:00	176
04:00	178
05:00	177
06:00	170
07:00	145
08:00	124
09:00	119
10:00	129
11:00	136
12:00	142
13:00	141
14:00	137
15:00	136
16:00	136

(continued)

Table 3.1   Continued

Hour (arrival)	Mean (average) duration to departure
17:00	140
18:00	142
19:00	145
20:00	152
21:00	157
22:00	163
23:00	169

Source: Office for National Statistics

These data are averages and unless assumptions are made about the distribution of the data it is not possible to infer what proportion exceeded the 4-hour target (this idea will be discussed in Chapter 6). However, an average of 226 minutes (3 hours 46 minutes) at midnight is very close to the target, so it is likely that many patients arriving at midnight will have a stay of longer than 4 hours. This data is also from all individual NHS Trusts in England, and some trusts will perform better than others (for example, Birmingham Children's Hospital NHS Foundation Trust achieved over 99%, while Surrey and Sussex Healthcare NHS Trust only achieved 81%).

The data supplied above only gives a partial view of length of stay in A&E. One statistic that would be useful is the range of the data. We will meet several statistics in this chapter that will help to define the average or typical value and its spread.

MEASURES OF LOCATION

I am sure that you have heard of the word 'average'. An average is some kind of representative item within a set of possible items. The word 'location' is used because, for numerical data, an average locates a typical value of some distribution. This is not as easy as it may seem as there could be several different values that would serve as this average figure.

Example 3.1

The number of sales made by two salespersons over the past few days has been as follows:

- Mike   3, 2, 1, 32, 2, 1, 1
- Janet   0, 1, 4, 12, 10, 7, 8, 6

What would be a good measure of the daily number of sales by each salesperson?

Six out of the seven values for Mike are between 1 and 3 sales per day, while for Janet the values are fairly evenly spread between 0 and 12 sales per day. Do you choose one of the existing values to represent the number of sales per day or do you choose a value that is in between?

There are in fact three different averages and each can give you different values. The next section defines each one and discusses the advantages and disadvantages of each.

The mean, median and mode

The *mean* ($\bar{x}$) is defined as the sum of all the values (x) divided by the total number of values (n). As a formula this is:

$$\bar{x} = \frac{\sum x}{n}$$

So for Mike the mean number of sales per day is:

$$\frac{3+2+1+32+2+1+1}{7} = 6$$

Notice that the mean is not one of the values in the set of data. (A mean value can also be a fractional value even if the data values are themselves whole numbers.)

You should also find that the mean for Janet is also 6. Looking at the two data sets you should realize that the mean is a good representative value for Janet as her data does not have any extreme values but not for Mike as the extreme value of 32 is clearly influencing the mean. The problem with the mean is that it gives equal importance to all values, including any extreme values.

The *median* overcomes this problem by choosing the middle value of a set of numbers. In order to find this value for Mike the data is first ordered in ascending order as follows:

1, 1, 1, 2, 2, 3, 32

The middle value of this set of 7 numbers is 2, which is a more typical value. In Janet's case you had an even set of numbers, so in this case you take the average of the middle two (6 and 7). The median for Janet is therefore 6.5.

The third average is the *mode* which is the most frequent occurring value. In Mike's data the most frequently occurring number is 1 so this is the mode. However, in Janet's the numbers are all different so this set of data does not have a mode.

The mode is most useful when you have categorical data. So if you did a travel to work survey and got the results shown in Table 3.2, you can see that the car is the most common method of travel.

Table 3.2   Results of a travel-to-work survey

Method of travel	Frequency
Car	9
Bus	4
Cycle	3
Walk	2
Train	2

The mean, median and mode for a frequency distribution

It is relatively straightforward finding an average of a small set of data, but when large quantities of data are involved, or when the data is supplied in the form of a frequency table, the methods of calculation become more involved.

Example 3.2

The ungrouped frequency table in Table 3.3 gives the daily number of sales made by the sales force of a double glazing company.

Table 3.3 Ungrouped frequency table

No. of Sales (x)	Frequency (f)
2	3
3	7
4	9
5	6
6	5
7	2
8	1

Table 3.4 Calculation of the mean for an ungrouped frequency table

No. of sales (x)	Frequency (f)	fx
2	3	6
3	7	21
4	9	36
5	6	30
6	5	30
7	2	14
8	1	8
Total	33	145

To find the mean you need to modify the basic formula for the mean as follows:

$$\bar{x} = \frac{\sum fx}{\sum f}$$

The calculations can be set out as in Table 3.4.

The mean is therefore $\frac{145}{33} = 4.4$ sales.

To find the median of the data in Table 3.3 you need to find the middle value. If you write down the cumulative frequencies as in Table 3.5 you will see that the middle value occurs at the 17th frequency which is when $x = 4$.

Table 3.5   Calculation of the median

x	f	Cumulative f
2	3	3
3	7	10
4	9	19
5	6	25
6	5	30
7	2	32
8	1	33

Table 3.6   Grouped frequency table

Interval	Frequency
30 to under 35 mm	4
35 to under 40 mm	7
40 to under 45 mm	14
45 to under 50 mm	23
50 to under 55 mm	16
55 to under 60 mm	9
60 to under 65 mm	4
65 to under 70 mm	1
70 to under 75 mm	1
75 to under 80 mm	0
80 to under 85 mm	1

To find the modal number of sales you need to find the sales that occur most frequently. This is 4 sales.

Example 3.3

The group frequency table shown in Table 3.6 refers to the length of 80 bolts produced by a machine.

This is a similar table to that in Example 3.2, except that x does not have a single value. In order to calculate the mean, the mid value is used for x.

So the mid value for the interval 30 to under 35 would be 32.5 (You can assume that you can get as close as you like to 35 mm). Table 3.7 shows how the mean is calculated by making x represent the midpoint of the range.

The mean is $\dfrac{3910}{80} = 48.875$.

The median can be found using Table 3.7 and the following equation:

$$\text{Median} = l + w\left(\frac{\dfrac{n}{2} - F}{f}\right)$$

where l is the lower boundary of the median group, w is the width of the median group, n is the number of values, f is the frequency in the median group and F is the cumulative frequency up to the median group. In our

Table 3.7 Calculation of the mean and median for a grouped frequency distribution

Interval	Midpoint (x)	Frequency f	fx	Cumulative frequency	% cumulative frequency
30 to under 35 mm	32.5	4	130.0	4	5.00
35 to under 40 mm	37.5	7	262.5	11	13.75
40 to under 45 mm	42.5	14	595.0	25	31.25
45 to under 50 mm	47.5	23	1092.5	48	60.00
50 to under 55 mm	52.5	16	840.0	64	80.00
55 to under 60 mm	57.5	9	517.5	73	91.25
60 to under 65 mm	62.5	4	250.0	77	96.25
65 to under 70 mm	67.5	1	67.5	78	97.50
70 to under 75 mm	72.5	1	72.5	79	98.75
75 to under 80 mm	77.5	0	0.0	79	98.75
80 to under 85 mm	82.5	1	82.5	80	100.00
	Total	80	3910.0		

example the median must be in the interval 45 to 50 mm so $l = 45$, $w = 5$, $n = 80$, $f = 23$ and $F = 25$. The median is therefore:

$$45 + 5 \left(\frac{\frac{80}{2} - 25}{23} \right) = 48.26 \text{ mm.}$$

The *modal class* of the data in Table 3.6 is 45 to 50 mm as this has the highest frequency. It is possible to estimate a single value for the mode using a graphical approach. This is shown in Figure 3.1 where you can see that the mode is approximately 48 mm. You might have noticed that all three averages are very similar. This is because the underlying distribution is approximately symmetrical. If the distribution were right-skewed the mean would be displaced to the right of the mode, and if the distribution were left-skewed the mean would be displaced to the left of the mode. The median is between the two but closer to the mean. Earnings data is a good example of a distribution that is right-skewed.

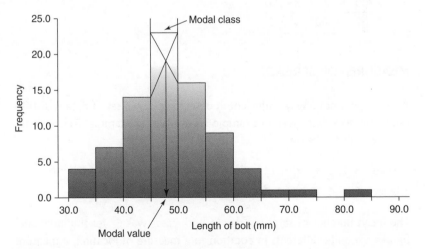

Figure 3.1 Graphical method for finding the mode

Table 3.8 Pay rise by category

Employee	Pay rise	No. of employees
Manual	1%	700
Clerical	3%	200
Management	8%	100

The weighted mean

In the calculation of the mean, each value was given an equal weighting. However, there are some circumstances where this is not correct. For example, Table 3.8 gives the pay rise given to 1000 employees.

The simple mean of the pay rise column is 4%. However, this ignores the fact that the majority of employees have received 3% or less. A fairer way would be to take the number of employees into account by *weighting* the pay rise by the number of employees in each category. The method is just like finding the mean of a grouped frequency table where frequency is the number of employees. The mean will therefore be:

$$\frac{1 \times 700 + 3 \times 200 + 8 \times 100}{1000} = 2.1\%$$

MEASURES OF SPREAD

An average is not always sufficient in describing how a set of data is distributed. The sales data given in Example 3.1 is a typical example. This data has been reproduced below.

- Mike   3, 2, 1, 32, 2, 1, 1
- Janet   0, 1, 4, 12, 10, 7, 8, 6

The mean number of sales per day in both cases was 6, yet the individual figures are quite different. In addition to a measure of location, a measure of *spread* or *dispersion* can also be provided. There are various measures of spread: the simplest is the *range*. The range is the difference between the smallest and largest and for Mike this is

32 – 1 = 31 sales per day, while for Janet it is 12 – 0 = 12. So there is a much larger spread in Mike's figures than in Janet's.

Unfortunately the range is too easily influenced by extreme values and is not a particularly good measure. Another measure is the *interquartile range* (IQR). To calculate the IQR the data is divided into quarters. If Q_1 is the lower quartile and Q_3 is the upper quartile, then

$$IQR = Q_3 - Q_1$$
(Q_2 is the median)

This method avoids the extremes and thus is more representative than the range. For example a survey by Commercial Motor in 2010 found that the mean salary of regional distribution centre managers (RDC) was £72,625, but 25% of managers were paid less than £60,900 and 25% were paid more than £82,438. The IQR is therefore £82,438 – £60,900 = £21,538. This figure could be compared with the salary of other professions to see if RDC managers have a larger spread of salaries and therefore more opportunities for advancement.

Although the IQR is an improvement on using the simple range, you are still only looking at the middle half of the data and ignoring the rest.

The variance and standard deviation

Another measure of spread is a statistic called the *variance* – this is a better measure as it uses all the data. The procedure for calculating the variance is:

1. Find the difference between each value and the mean.
2. Square this difference (this removes the negative signs).
3. Add up all these squared differences.
4. Divide the total squared difference by one less than the number of data items (n).

The reason for dividing by $n - 1$ and not n has to do with the fact that when you take a sample of data items the spread will be less than the spread of the population. To understand this, think of how many seven-foot people you know. There will be several seven-foot people in a country, and the spread of heights of the population will be influenced by these people. Yet if you take only a small sample, it is extremely unlikely that you will get any very tall or very short people, so the sample spread will be less than the population spread. Dividing by $n - 1$ helps to compensate for this. This adjustment is only really important for small sample sizes (n below 30). We will come back to this issue when we look at sample data in Chapter 6.

The variance is one of the most important measures in statistics. However, as it is in squared units, it is usual to use the square root of the answer: this statistic is called the *standard deviation* and has the same units as the data. Standard deviation is a far more practical measure of spread and will be used extensively throughout this text.

The variance not only takes account of all data values but also magnifies the effect of values that are a long way from the mean. Data that is more spread out will have a larger variance than data that is clustered closer to the mean.

The procedure for calculating the variance for Mike's sales is shown in Table 3.9. Remember that the mean was 6.

Table 3.9   Calculation of the variance for Mike's sales

Sales x	Difference $x-6$	Difference squared $(x-6)^2$
3	−3	9
2	−4	16
1	−5	25
32	26	676
2	−4	16
1	−5	25
1	−5	25
	Total	792

Variance $= \dfrac{792}{7-1} = 132.0$

The variance is usually represented by the symbol s^2

$S^2 = 132$

The standard deviation, s, is $\sqrt{132} = 11.5$ sales per day

Notice how the variance is affected by the outlier of 32 sales.

In algebraic terms the formula for the variance is:

$$s^2 = \frac{\sum(x - \bar{x})^2}{n-1}$$

The problems with this formula are that it is tedious and can be inaccurate if the mean has been rounded. A better formula is:

$$s^2 = \frac{\sum x^2 - \dfrac{(\sum x)^2}{n}}{n-1}$$

This formula and Table 3.10 will be used to calculate the standard deviation of Janet's sales data.

Table 3.10 Calculation of the variance of Janet's data

	x	x^2
	0	0
	1	1
	4	16
	12	144
	10	100
	7	49
	8	64
	6	36
Total	48	410

$$s^2 = \frac{410 - \frac{(48)^2}{8}}{7}$$

$$s^2 = \frac{122}{7}$$

$$= 17.4$$

and the standard deviation, $s = 4.2$ sales per day.

This calculation demonstrates that compared to Mike, Janet has a much smaller variation in her daily number of sales.

The variance and standard deviation for a frequency distribution

A slightly different formula is used for a frequency distribution to reflect the fact that frequencies are involved. The formula normally used for the variance is:

$$s^2 = \frac{\sum fx^2}{\sum f} - \left(\frac{\sum fx}{\sum f}\right)^2$$

Using this formula and Table 3.11 we can calculate the variance and standard deviation of the bolt length data (Example 3.3).

The variance is therefore:

$$\frac{197350}{80} - \left(\frac{3910}{80}\right)^2 = 2466.875 - 2388.7656$$

$$s^2 = 78.1$$

And the standard deviation:

$$s = \sqrt{78.1}$$

$$= 8.8 \text{ mm}$$

Table 3.11   Calculation of the standard deviation for the bolt length data

Interval	x	f	fx	x^2	fx^2
30 to under 35 mm	32.5	4	130.0	1056.25	4255.00
35 to under 40 mm	37.5	7	262.5	1406.25	9843.75
40 to under 45 mm	42.5	14	595.0	1806.25	25827.50
45 to under 50 mm	47.5	23	1092.5	2256.25	51893.25
50 to under 55 mm	52.5	16	840.0	2756.25	44100.00
55 to under 60 mm	57.5	9	517.5	3306.25	29756.25
60 to under 65 mm	62.5	4	250.0	3906.25	15625.00
65 to under 70 mm	67.5	1	67.5	4556.25	4556.25
70 to under 75 mm	72.5	1	72.5	5256.25	5256.25
75 to under 80 mm	77.5	0	0.0	6006.25	0.00
80 to under 85 mm	82.5	1	82.5	6806.25	6806.25
	Total	80	3910.0	39118.75	197350.00

COEFFICIENT OF VARIATION

If two sets of data have similar means then it is easy to compare the variation by calculating their standard deviations. However, if the means are very different then the comparisons of spread will not be so obvious. The solution is to calculate the ratio of the mean to the standard deviation and is usually expressed as a percentage. This is called the coefficient of variation. For example suppose you are comparing the reliability of two types of machines. Machine A has mean time to breakdown of 12.2 weeks with a standard deviation of 3.5 weeks, while the equivalent statistics for machine B is 9 months and 1.5 months, respectively. Which machine has the highest variability?

(a) Machine A Coefficient of variation = $\dfrac{3.5}{12.2} \times 100 = 28.7\%$

(b) Machine B Coefficient of variation = $\dfrac{1.5}{9.0} \times 100 = 16.7\%$

So machine A has the largest variation.

BOX AND WHISKER PLOTS

A very useful diagram that summarizes information about the location and spread of a set of data is the *box and whisker* plot. The 'box' represents the middle 50% of the data and the extremities of the box are the quartiles Q_1 and Q_3. The median (Q_2) is marked and will obviously be inside the box. Each 'whisker' represents 25% of the data, and the extremities of the whiskers are the minimum and upper values of the data (or the class intervals). Figure 3.2 shows the box and whisker plot for bolt length data given in Example 3.3.

Not only does this diagram give you an idea of the average and spread, it also tells you about the shape of the distribution of the data. If the box is small compared to the whiskers this indicates a distribution that is bunched in the middle with long tails. A box shifted to one side or the other indicates skewness, as does the position of the median within the box. In the case of the bolt lengths the right-hand whisker is slightly longer than the left, suggesting a slight right skewness to the distribution. However, the median is close to the middle of the box so this skewness is small. The box and whisker plot is particularly useful when you have two or more distributions to compare.

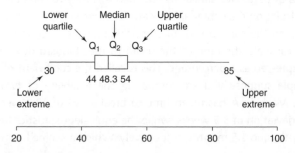

Figure 3.2 Box and whisker plot

KEY POINTS

★ The mean, median and mode are measures of average; they locate the data.

★ In a symmetrical distribution, the mean, median and mode are equal. In a right-skewed distribution the mean and median are greater than the mode, and in a left-skewed distribution they are less than the mode.

★ To describe a set of data fully, a measure of spread is required. The range is the simplest measure, but a better measure is the interquartile range (IQR). The IQR uses the middle 50 per cent of the data and is therefore less influenced by extreme values. The best measure of spread is the variance. The square root of the variance is the standard deviation, which is in the same units as the data.

★ When comparing the spread of two or more distributions, it is useful to compare the coefficients of variation for each as these take into account differences in the mean. A good visual summary of a frequency distribution is a box and whisker plot. This diagram can be used to compare several different distributions side by side.

FURTHER READING

Most texts on quantitative methods and all elementary statistical texts will have a chapter on descriptive statistics. Chapter 5 in Oakshott (2012) gives a similar treatment and also includes details of how to use Excel and SPSS. Straight Statistics and Sense about Science have produced a very useful free publication called *Making Sense of Statistics*. The pdf of this publication can be downloaded at *www.straightstatistics.org/resources/making-sense-statistics*. Another very interesting text and in the same vein is *The Tiger that Isn't: Seeing through a World of Numbers* by Blastland and Dilnot (2007). Both these publications look at statistics from a commonsense perspective and show how statistics can often deceive unless we know what to look for.

REVISION QUESTIONS

1 The weekly gross pay of 5 employees was as follows:

£160.24, £183.56, £155.00, £274.50, £174.34

(a) Calculate the mean and median of the data. Which average may be more appropriate, and why?

(b) Calculate the standard deviation of the data.

2 Which average(s) is most appropriate in each case?

(a) The test scores of a class of students

(b) The earnings of people in a particular industry

(c) The weights of pre-packed food

(d) Shoes stocked by a shoe shop

(e) Sizes of parts produced by a machine

3 Table 3.12 shows the number of rejects from a production process. Find the mean and standard deviation.

4 Items are manufactured to the same nominal length on two different machines, A and B. A number of items from each machine are measured and the results are shown in Table 3.13.

(a) Find the mean, median and modal values for the two machines.

(b) Find the interquartile range and standard deviation for both machines.

(c) Calculate the coefficient of variation for both machines.

(d) Draw a box and whisker plot for both machines.

(e) Use your results from (a) to (d) to comment on the lengths of items produced by both machines.

Table 3.12 Number of rejects from a production process

Number of rejects	Frequency
0	12
1	45
2	36
3	30
4	20
5	5
6	0

Table 3.13 Data for Question 4

Class interval (mm)	Frequency	
	Machine A	Machine B
20 to under 22	5	2
22 to under 24	12	5
24 to under 26	26	20
26 to under 28	11	25
28 to under 30	3	8
30 to under 32	0	2

4
INDEX NUMBERS

OBJECTIVES

- To be able to calculate a simple one-item index
- To be able to calculate the Laspeyres' index
- To be able to calculate the Paasche's index
- To understand the differences between the RPI and CPI

INTRODUCTION

An index is a means of comparing changes in some variable, often price over time. This is particularly useful when there are many items involved and when the prices and quantities are in different units. The best-known index in the UK is the retail price index (RPI) although the consumer price index (CPI) is becoming more prominent now that it is the official measure of inflation when it comes to up-rating public sector pensions and benefits. Both indices compare the price of a 'basket' of goods from one month to another. This chapter looks at the construction and use of different types of indices.

OUTPUT OF THE PRODUCTION INDUSTRIES

The Office for National Statistics in the UK collects and publishes large amounts of statistics on a whole range of economic and demographic factors such as unemployment, production and cost of goods. One purpose of the statistics is to see how the UK is doing relative to previous years. The easiest way to do this is by using index numbers. Table 4.1 is an example of production data in the UK, and each year is compared to 2008 which has been given an index of 100 and is called the *base year*. As you can see the index for all production industries has fallen below 100 after 2008, which means that production has fallen. So we don't need the actual production figures to compare one year from the base. Percentage change has also been calculated and this compares the current year with the previous one. Looking at this table you will also notice that there is a row labelled 'Latest weight'. This is because production industries are made up of a number of different sectors such as manufacturing and oil and gas extraction. Each of these sectors will contribute a different amount to the overall figures, and so each sector is weighted according to its importance. This idea is explained later in this chapter.

Table 4.1 Output of the production industries

IOP5 Output of the production industries
Chained volume indices of gross value added

| | Broad industry groups | | | | | |
	Production industries	Mining and quarrying	Manu-facturing	Electricity, gas, steam and air conditioning	Water supply, sewerage and waste management	Oil and gas extraction
Section	B+C+D+E	B	C	D	E	06
Latest weight	1000.0	164.3	665.7	93.2	76.8	140.5
	K222	K224	K22A	K248	K24C	K226

(continued)

Table 4.1 Continued

	Broad industry groups					
	Production industries	Mining and quarrying	Manu-facturing	Electricity, gas, steam and air conditioning	Water supply, sewerage and waste management	Oil and gas extraction
Section	B+C+D+E	B	C	D	E	06
2006	102.4	109.7	101.9	98.7	98.8	108.7
2007	102.9	107.0	102.7	99.5	101.8	106.1
2008	100.0	100.0	100.0	100.0	100.0	100.0
2009	91.0	91.0	90.4	95.2	91.9	91.8
2010	92.7	86.5	93.7	98.6	90.4	85.9
Percentage change, latest year on previous year						
2006	–	−7.6	1.7	−0.3	−2.7	−9.6
2007	0.5	−2.5	0.8	0.8	3.0	−2.4
2008	−2.8	−6.5	−2.6	0.5	−1.8	−5.8
2009	−9.0	−9.0	−9.6	−4.8	−8.1	−8.2
2010	1.9	−4.9	3.7	3.5	−1.6	−6.5

Source: Office for National Statistics

SIMPLE INDICES

Looking at Table 4.1 from the case study we see that in 2008 the index is 100. This is called the *base year*. To obtain the index in subsequent years we simply divide the actual value of production from that year by the actual value of production in the base year and multiply the answer by 100. As a formula, this is

$$\frac{p_n}{p_0} \times 100$$

Where p_n represents the value at year n and p_0 represents the value at the base year.

Example 4.1

The average weekly pay in the UK in January 2000 was £311 and this had risen to £445 by January 2010 (Source: Office for National Statistics). If we make the base year 2000 then $p_0 = 311$ and $p_n = 445$ and the earnings index for 2010 is

$$\frac{445}{311} \times 100 = 143.1$$

This shows that the average weekly pay has increased by 43.1% from 2000 to 2010.

WEIGHTED AGGREGATE INDICES

Example 4.2

The resources used in the manufacture of glass-fibre boats include resin, glass-fibre mat and labour. The price of each of these resources varies and the average price during each of the years from 2011 to 2013 is shown in Table 4.2.

If we make 2011 the base year we could calculate the index for each resource for each year. The result is shown in Table 4.3 below (the calculations are left as an exercise for the reader).

Table 4.2   Price data for the production of glass-fibre boats

Item	2011	2012	2013
Resin	£0.25/l	£0.20/l	£0.18/l
Mat	£0.16/m^2	£0.16/m^2	£0.20/m^2
Labour	£6.08	£6.19	£6.31

Table 4.3 Price index

Item	2011	2012	2013
Resin	100	80	72
Mat	100	100	125
Labour	100	101.8	103.8

Table 4.4 Quantity data for the production of glass-fibre boats

Item	2011	2012	2013
Resin	50 *l*	48 *l*	48 *l*
Mat	200 m^2	210 m^2	215 m^2
Labour	30 hours	27 hours	23 hours

From this table we can see that the index for resin has shown a decrease while glass-fibre mat has shown the greatest increase. But how has the cost of production in total changed? What we need is an overall index but because each resource is in different units it would be difficult to combine them. There is also the problem that the importance of each resource may well be different. For instance labour is likely to be the dominant cost to the company. To overcome these problems each item is weighted according to its importance. One way of measuring importance is to record the quantities used in production (see Table 4.4).

Since price × quantity equals the cost of that item, the *aggregate* index could be obtained as:

$$\frac{Total\ cost\ of\ production\ at\ current\ prices}{Total\ cost\ of\ production\ at\ base\ year\ prices}$$

There is, however, one problem with this definition. What quantities should we use? Both price and quantities have varied from year to year and for comparison purposes we need to use the same quantities for the numerator and denominator of the index. The choice is to use either the base year quantities or the current year quantities. When you use the former you have a base-weighted or *Laspeyres'* index, and when you use the latter you have a current weighted or *Paasche's* index.

Laspeyres' index

The definition of the Laspeyres' index is:

$$\frac{Total\ cost\ of\ base\ year\ quantities\ at\ current\ prices}{Total\ cost\ of\ base\ year\ quantities\ at\ base\ year\ prices}$$

Using p to represent price and q to represent quantity, this definition can expressed as:

$$\frac{\Sigma p_n q_0}{\Sigma p_0 q_0} \times 100$$

The calculation for the boat example is shown in Table 4.5.

So the Laspeyres' index for 2013 is:

$$\frac{238.3}{226.9} \times 100 = 105.0$$

Paasche's index

The definition of the Paasche's index is:

$$\frac{Total\ cost\ of\ current\ year\ quantities\ at\ current\ prices}{Total\ cost\ of\ current\ year\ quantities\ at\ base\ year\ prices}$$

Table 4.5 Calculation of Laspeyres' index for 2013

	P_0	q_0	P_n	$P_0 q_0$	$P_n q_0$
Resin	0.25	50	0.18	12.5	9
Mat	0.16	200	0.20	32.0	40.0
Labour	6.08	30	6.31	182.4	189.3
			Sum	226.9	238.3

This can again be expressed in algebraic form as:

$$\frac{\Sigma p_n q_n}{\Sigma p_0 q_n} \times 100$$

Again using a table method of calculating Paasche's index.

So the Paasche's index for 2013 is:

$$\frac{196.77}{186.24} \times 100 = 105.7$$

Both indices give similar results for this data and in general there will not be a great difference between the two unless the weights (quantities) are very different

In practice the Laspeyres' index is the most commonly used index and the base year is redefined at regular intervals.

Table 4.6 Calculation of Paasche's index for 2013

	P_0	q_n	P_n	$P_0 q_n$	$P_n q_n$
Resin	0.25	48	0.18	12.0	8.64
Mat	0.16	215	0.20	34.4	43.0
Labour	6.08	23	6.31	139.84	145.13
			Sum	186.24	196.77

CONSUMER PRICE INDICES

Two very important indices are the retail price index (RPI) and the consumer price index (CPI). They both show how prices have changed (usually upwards!) over the years and are a determining factor in deciding how interest rates, wages, pensions and tax allowances for instance are changed. Both indices measure the change in the price of a 'basket' of goods and are used as a measure of inflation although the government inflation target is based in the CPI. The RPI covers some 650 items divided into 14 groups, such as food, housing and motoring expenditure. Each component of the index is given a weight to represent the importance of that item and the weights are updated annually by the family expenditure survey. Prices of each item in the index are checked monthly. The weights used in the RPI are designed for the 'average' family and are not representative of high income groups or pensioners. The CPI is similar but excludes things like council tax and other housing costs, but its weights cover all income groups. It also include some financial services and follows international definitions.

KEY POINTS

★ An index allows changes in a variable to be compared over a period of time.

★ The base index is given a value of 100, so an index value below 100 means a decrease and a value above 100 means an increase. As the base is 100, these changes can also be expressed in percentage terms.

★ For a single item or variable, a simple index can be used.

★ Where several items are involved, it is necessary to use a weighted aggregate index. There are two main weighted indices. These are Laspeyres' index, which is a base-weighted index, and Paasche's index, which is a current-weighted index.

★ The Laspeyres' index is easier to use but soon gets out of date, while the Paasche's index reflects consumption patterns in the current year.

★ The retail price index (RPI) and consumer price index (CPI) use consumption patterns as weights. These are derived from a family expenditure survey.

★ The RPI and CPI are used as measures of inflation. The CPI is the index favoured by the UK government and is used to up-rate public sector pensions and benefits.

FURTHER READING

Most general quantitative method texts have a chapter on index numbers. Chapter 2 in Oakshott (2012) gives a similar treatment to this text. The text by Curwin and Slater (2008) gives a good coverage, particularly on the differences between RPI and CPI. There are many online sources, particularly from the Office of National Statistics (ONS). The ONS website for all sources of economic data including the RPI and CPI is www.ons.gov.uk.

REVISION QUESTIONS

1 Labour costs (in £000s) for an engineering company over the last 10 years has been as follows

2002	2003	2004	2005	2006	2007	2008	2009	2010	2011
50.1	65.3	68.6	72.0	76.6	78.3	88.7	90.5	99.3	112.9

Convert these costs into an index using 2002 as the base year.

2 A manufacturer of greeting cards requires ink, card and production staff to produce its range of cards. The estimated cost of each resource over the past 3 years is as follows:

Resource	2009	2010	2011
Ink (£ per litre)	£0.55	£0.58	£0.76
Card (£ per m²)	£0.05	£0.05	£0.08
Labour (£ per hour)	£6.50	£6.90	£7.00

The quantity of each resource used over the same time period is as follows:

Resource	2009	2010	2011
Ink (litres)	4000	5000	3000
Card (m²)	115 000	124 000	110 000
Labour (number)	25	34	30

(a) Calculate the Laspeyres' index for 2010 and 2011 using 2009 as the base year

(b) Calculate the Paasche's index for 2010 and 2011 using 2009 as the base year

(c) Comment on the change in both indices over the 3 years.

3 The price and quantity consumed in a normal week of 3 items of food for a family are as follows:

| | 1990 | | 2010 | |
	Price	Quantity	Price	Quantity
Bread	28p/loaf	6 loaves	78p/loaf	6 loaves
Milk	20p/litre	15 litres	50p/litre	12 litres
Tea	96p/packet	1 packet	75p/packet	2 packets

(a) Calculate the Laspeyres' index for 2010 using 1990 as the base year.

(b) Calculate the Paasche's index for 2010 using 1990 as the base year.

5
APPLICATIONS OF PROBABILITY

OBJECTIVES

- To be able to calculate simple probabilities
- To be able to calculate probabilities of compound events using the rules of addition and multiplication
- To know how to use probability trees to solve problems
- To understand how to apply Bayes' theorem to modify probabilities when new information is received
- To be able to calculate expected monetary values
- To know how to solve problems using decision trees

INTRODUCTION

It is difficult to go very far in solving business problems without a basic understanding of probability. The 'laws of chance' underpin many decisions that are made in real life. For example, when we carry out a survey we need to know how the sample data relate to the target population. Our insurance premiums are determined by the chance of some mishap occurring, and quality control systems are built around probability laws. Trading in stocks and shares also relies on an understanding of probability. There are also many games of chance, including card and dice games, horse racing and the National Lottery. This chapter contains all the basic rules and methods of probability that will be required in subsequent chapters. It also looks at one important application; that is, decision-making under conditions of uncertainty.

London International Financial Futures and Options Exchange (LIFFE)

By its very nature the stock market is volatile with share prices constantly changing. However it is not completely random and a billion-pound industry exists to try and beat the market. Investors can make a lot of money by correctly predicting the market more than 50% of the time. However as was demonstrated in 2008 the consequences of getting things wrong can be disastrous!

Stock market investment therefore has an element of risk as we cannot be sure that our predictions will be correct. In other words the probability that we correctly predict the market is much less than 100%. Large institutions try and spread this risk by investing in different stocks or investment types. Some people or organizations are risk seekers as they like the gamble and the chance of making a large return. Others are risk averse and prefer to invest in 'safe' investments such as fixed rate bonds.

Building societies are one part of the financial sector that should not take large risks. At one time they simply lent money at a variable rate of interest and borrowed money at variable rate of interest. So if they had to pay more to borrow money they simply increased the interest rate to borrowers. However, since the opening up of competition in the mortgage market, building societies now have to offer fixed rate mortgages and fixed rate deals to lenders. To *hedge* against possible interest rate rises building societies now use the London International Financial Futures and Options Exchange (LIFFE) to purchase interest rate futures. This allows the institution to buy a contract that essentially pays out for every percentage rate rise in interest rates. Of course if the interest rate falls then they pay the seller of the future a corresponding amount of money. However this is covered by the fact that they have to pay out less interest to borrowers. In this way building societies have taken the risk out of their business. LIFFE also allows future trading in equities and commodities. LIFFE is now part of the New York Stock Exchange (NSE).

Source: The Times 100 Business Case Studies

BASIC IDEAS

The value of a probability can be given either as a fraction, as a decimal or as a percentage. An event with a probability of zero is termed impossible, while an event with a probability of 1 or 100% is termed certain. Figure 5.1 may help you to picture the idea of the probability measure.

Probabilities can be obtained in a number of ways. The simplest is the *subjective* method where you estimate what you think the probability of a

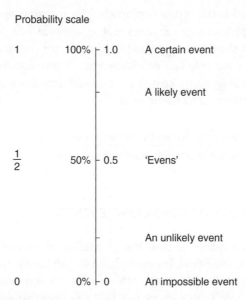

Figure 5.1 Probability scale

particular event will be. For example, a sales manager may estimate that the probability of high sales for a particular product is 60%. This figure may be based on market research or experience of a similar product, but it is unlikely to involve any calculations. Another method is the *empirical* approach. This method uses measurement to estimate probabilities. For example, you may wish to determine the probability of a defective electrical component being produced by a particular process. If you test 100 components and find 5 defective, then you would say that the probability of a defective component being produced is 5/100 or 0.05. That is

$$\text{Probability} = \frac{\text{number of times a particular event has occurred}}{\text{total number of trials or 'experiments'}}$$

The particular event here is finding a defective component and the 'experiment' is picking, testing and classifying a component as either good or defective.

Another method is the *a priori* approach. This is similar to the empirical approach except that you can work out in advance how many times a particular event should occur. If you tossed a coin the probability of a head is 0.5 since there are only two possible events. If you picked a card from a pack, the probability of an Ace is 4/52 or 0.0769 since there are four aces in a pack. The definition can be written as:

$$\frac{\text{number of ways in which an event can occur}}{\text{total number of possible outcomes}}$$

THE PROBABILITY OF COMPOUND EVENTS

It is frequently required to find the probability of two or more events happening at the same time. For example, an aircraft has many of its controls duplicated so that if one fails the other would still function. But what is the probability that both systems will fail? The way that probabilities are combined depends on whether the events are independent or whether they are mutually exclusive. Two (or more) events are said to be independent if the occurrence of one does not affect the occurrence of the other. The two aircraft systems will be independent if the failure of one system does not change the probability of failure of the other system. Two (or more) events are mutually exclusive if either event can occur, but not both. One card drawn from a pack cannot be a Jack and an Ace. However, a Jack and a Diamond are not mutually exclusive since the selected card could be both. When the set of all possible outcomes are known, they are said to be mutually exhaustive, and the sum of the probabilities of a set of outcomes that are mutually exclusive and mutually exhaustive must equal 1. For example, there are four suits in a pack of cards and the probability of selecting a card from a given suit is 13/52 or 0.25. The sum of these probabilities is 1, since a card must come from one (and only one) of the suits. This idea will allow you to calculate a probability if the other or others are known. If, say, the probability of a defective component is 5%, then the probability that it is not defective is 95%.

Compound events can be more easily solved if a diagram is drawn. One useful diagram is the *Venn* diagram. A Venn diagram is made up of a square, the inside of which encloses all possible outcomes. The events of interest are represented by circles. The Venn diagram in Figure 5.2 represents two events, A and B. Event A is being dealt a Jack, which has a probability of 4/52 or 0.0769 and Event B is being dealt an Ace which also has a probability of 4/52. The probability of being dealt either a Jack or an Ace is:

$$P(\text{Jack or Ace}) = P(\text{Jack}) + P(\text{Ace})$$
$$= 0.0769 + 0.0769$$
$$= 0.1538$$

However, if Event B is being dealt a Diamond then the two events overlap, as shown in Figure 5.3. If the two probabilities are now added, the intersection of the two events (shown shaded) will have been added twice. This intersection, which represents the case of being dealt a Jack of Diamonds

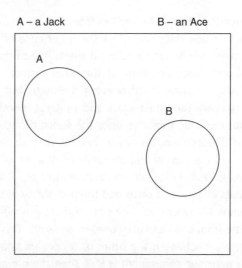

A – a Jack   B – an Ace

Figure 5.2 Venn diagram for mutually exclusive events

(with a probability of 1/52 or 0.0192), must be subtracted from the sum of the two probabilities. That is:

P(Jack or Diamond) = P(Jack) + P(Diamond) – P(Jack of Diamonds)

$$= 0.0769 + 0.25 – 0.0192$$

$$= 0.3077$$

In general if P(A) means the probability of Event A and P(B) the probability of Event B then:

P(A or B) = P(A) + P(B) – P(A and B)

This is known as the *addition rule*.

NOTE: If the two events are mutually exclusive, as in the first example, then there is no intersection and P(A and B) is zero.

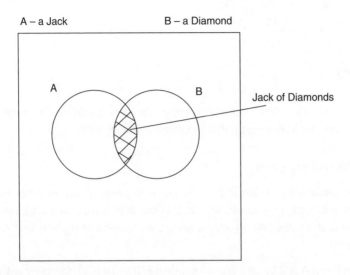

A – a Jack   B – a Diamond

A   B   Jack of Diamonds

Figure 5.3 Venn diagram for events that are not mutually exclusive

Table 5.1 Results from checks on heavy goods vehicles

	Overweight	Not overweight	Total
Driving time exceeded	15	25	40
Driving time not exceeded	20	40	60
Total	35	65	100

For example Table 5.1 shows the results from checks on 100 heavy goods vehicles.

Assuming that this data is typical of all heavy goods vehicles on the road we can calculate the probability that if a vehicle was stopped at random it would either be overweight or the driver had exceeded the allowed driving time.

Since it is possible for both the vehicle to be overweight and the driver to have exceeded the driving time, the events are not mutually exclusive. Using the addition law we get:

P(time exceeded or overweight) = P(time exceeded) + P(overweight)
                                – P(time exceeded and overweight)

$$= \frac{40}{100} + \frac{35}{100} - \frac{15}{100}$$

$$= 0.6$$

That is, there is a 60% chance that either the lorry would be overweight or the driver would have exceeded the driving time or both.

Conditional probability

If the probability of Event B occurring is dependent on whether Event A has occurred, you would say that Event B is conditional on Event A. This is written $P(B \mid A)$ which means the probability of B given that A has occurred.

When Event A and Event B are independent $P(B \mid A) = P(B)$. Sampling without replacement is a good example of conditional probability. If two students are to be chosen randomly from a group of 5 girls and 4 boys, then the probability that the first person is a girl is 5/9 or 0.5556 and the probability that it is a boy is $1 - 0.5556 = 0.4444$. The probability that the second person is a girl depends on the outcome of the first choice.

First choice	Probability of second choice being a girl
Boy	5/8 or 0.625
Girl	4/8 or 0.5

If you want to know the probability of the first student being a girl and the second student being a girl, you will need to use the multiplication rule. If the events are dependent, as in this example, the rule is:

$P(A \text{ and } B) = P(A) \times P(B \mid A)$

So $P(\text{girl and a girl}) = 0.5556 \times 0.5 = 0.2778$.

If two (or more) events are independent the rule simplifies to: $P(A \text{ and } B) = P(A) \times P(B)$

For example, if an aircraft has a main and a back-up computer and the probability of failure of either computer is 1%, then the probability of both failing is

$0.01 \times 0.01 = 0.0001$ or 0.01%.

Tree diagrams

A very useful diagram to use when solving compound events, particularly when conditional probability is involved, is the tree diagram. This diagram represents different outcomes of an experiment by means of branches. For example, in the student example the two 'experiments' of choosing an individual can be represented by the tree diagram in Figure 5.4. The first experiment is represented by a small circle or node, and the two possible outcomes are represented by branches radiating out from the node. The event and probability are written alongside the branch. The second experiment is again represented by a node and you will notice that this node appears twice, once for each outcome of the first experiment. Branches again radiate out from each node, but notice that the probability is different depending on what happened in the first experiment.

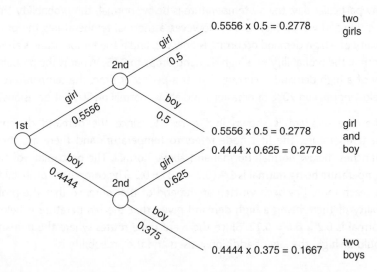

Figure 5.4 A tree diagram

You will see that the compound events have been written at the end of each route in Figure 5.4. If you add up these probabilities you will see that they sum to 1 (to 3 decimal places). This is because the routes are mutually exclusive and mutually exhaustive. They are mutually exclusive because one and only one of the routes can be followed, and they are mutually exhaustive because all possible routes have been shown. From this diagram various probabilities could be evaluated using the law of addition. For example, the probability of getting two students of the same sex is

0.2778 + 0.1667 = 0.4445.

It is unlikely that you would use a tree diagram to solve a simple problem like this, but consider the problem in Example 5.1.

Example 5.1

The demand for gas is dependent on the weather and much research has been undertaken to forecast the demand accurately. This is important since it is quite difficult (and expensive) to increase the supply at short notice. If, on any particular day, the air temperature is below normal, the probability that the demand will be high is 0.6. However, at normal temperatures the probability of a high demand occurring is only 0.2, and if the temperature is above normal the probability of a high demand drops to 0.05. What is the probability of a high demand occurring if, over a period of time, the temperature is below normal on 20% of occasions and above normal on 30% of occasions?

The tree diagram is shown in Figure 5.5. Since the demand depends on temperature, the first node refers to temperature and there are three branches: below normal, normal and above normal. The probability of the temperature being normal is 1 − (0.2 + 0.3) = 0.5. The compound probability for each route has been written at the end of the route, so that the probability of there being a high demand given that the temperature is below normal is 0.2 × 0.6 = 0.12. Since there are three routes where the demand could be high, the law of addition is used and the probability is:

0.12 + 0.10 + 0.015 = 0.235

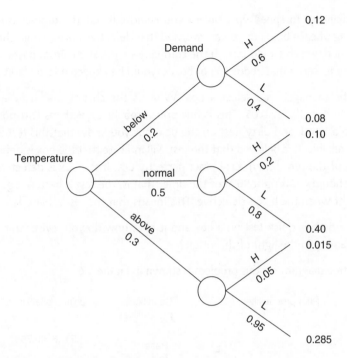

Figure 5.5 Tree diagram for temperature and demand for gas (Example 5.1)

Bayes' theorem

This theorem is based on the idea that in many situations we begin an analysis with some *prior* or initial probability estimate for the event we are interested in. This probability can come from historical data, previous experience, a pilot survey, and so on.

Then, we receive additional information from a survey, test, report, and so on, so that we are able to update our prior probability and calculate, using Bayes' theorem, what is known as our *posterior probability*. Consider Example 5.2

Example 5.2

You are a manager of a company that manufactures 'set top' boxes for digital TV. There is a large demand for these boxes and retailers are urgently asking for delivery. To speed up delivery you could cut out the time-consuming testing of each box, but you are worried that defective boxes would then be returned, which would tarnish the company's reputation. From past experience you know that about 5% of boxes would be expected to be faulty.

As the manager, you select a box. What is the chance that it is faulty? Clearly it is 5% or 0.05. This is our prior probability. Perhaps it is possible to do a 'quick and dirty' test on the box, but you know that this test is not very reliable. It is believed that the test will indicate that the box is defective 20% of the time when it is in fact perfectly OK. If the box is defective the test should get it right 90% of the time; that is, the test is better at getting it right when the box is defective. This means that the test is biased.

If you do this quick test on a box and it fails, how do you revise your prior probability in the light of this result?

The tree diagram for this problem is shown in Figure 5.6

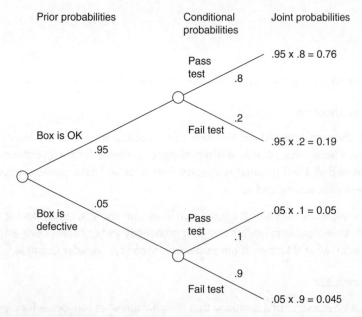

Figure 5.6 Calculation of joint probabilities

The probability of the test being correct or not is the *conditional* probability as it is conditional on the first branch of the tree. The probabilities at the end of the tree are the *joint* probabilities as they are obtained by multiplying the prior and conditional probabilities together. The probability that a box would fail the test is the sum of the relevant joint probabilities; that is, 0.19 + 0.045 = 0.235. The probability that the box is defective given that it failed the test is called the posterior probability, and for our problem it is:

$$\frac{0.045}{0.235} = 0.1915$$

Bayes' theorem can be expressed using the following equation:

$$P(B \mid A) = \frac{P(B \text{ and } A)}{P(A)}$$

In our example B is the event 'box is defective' and A is the event 'it failed the test'.

Bayes' theorem is a very powerful technique in solving probability problems, and we will come back to an important application of this theorem when we look at decision trees later in this chapter.

Expected value

If you toss a coin 100 times, you would expect 50 heads and 50 tails. That is, the expected number of heads is 0.5 × 100 = 50. In general it is a long-run average, which means it is the value you would get if you repeated the experiment long enough. It is calculated by multiplying a value of a particular variable by the probability of its occurrence and repeating this for all possible values. In symbols this can be represented as:

Expected value = $\sum px$

where $\sum$ means the 'sum of'.

Expected value is most often used for financial transactions. In this case it is usually referred to as *expected monetary value* or EMV. For example suppose a stock market investor buys £1000 of shares with the object of making a capital gain after 1 year. She believes that there is a 5% chance that the shares will double in value, a 25% chance that they will be worth £1500, a 30% chance that they will only be worth £500 and a 40% chance that they will not change in value. The expected monetary value of this investment, ignoring dealing costs:

$$= 0.05 \times 2000 + 0.25 \times 1500 + 0.30 \times 500 + 0.4 \times 1000 = £1025$$

DECISION TREES

When we need to make business decisions under conditions of uncertainty we often use a decision tree to help make the problem clearer and to enable us to make a rational choice between the different alternatives. Most often these decisions are *multi-stage* in that one decision leads to another. Decision trees are like probability trees except that as well as probabilistic branches there are also decision branches. The skeleton of a single-stage decision tree is shown in Figure 5.7

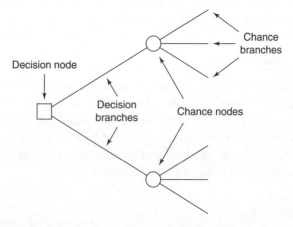

Figure 5.7 Decision tree

The square node represents the point where the decision is made, while the round nodes represent the point at which chance takes over. The decision tree is drawn from left to right, but to evaluate the tree you work from right to left. This is called the *roll back* method. You first evaluate the EMV at each chance node and then at the decision node you select the 'best' EMV (don't forget, 'best' can be lowest cost as well as largest profit).

Example 5.3

The Delma Oil Company has obtained government approval to drill for oil in the Baltic Sea. This area is known to contain oil deposits and industry sources believe that there is a 50% chance that oil will be found in a commercially viable quantity. The cost of the drilling programme is believed to be £30m, but this could be more than offset by the potential revenue, which is put at £100m at today's prices.

The company could carry out test drillings at different sites, which would only cost £5m. From historical data, tests are likely to indicate a viable field 65% of the time. However, these tests are not completely reliable and the probability that they are correct is only 0.7. That is, if the tests are positive there is a 70% chance that a viable quantity of oil will be found, and if negative there is only a 30% (100 – 70) chance that oil will be found in a viable quantity.

The company could sell its rights to drill in the area, but the revenue obtained will depend on the outcome of the tests (if carried out) and are as follows:

- Tests indicate oil £35m
- Tests don't indicate oil £3m
- No tests carried out £10m

This is a two-stage decision problem. The first decision is whether to test drill and the second decision is whether to start a drilling programme. In order to solve this decision problem you would carry out the following three steps.

Step 1

Draw the decision tree. This is shown in Figure 5.8. You will see that the decision nodes have been numbered 1, 2 and 3, while the chance nodes have been labelled as a, b, c and d. The values at the end of each branch of the tree represent the net outcome. For instance, if drilling is carried out without any tests and oil is found, the net outcome is a profit of £100m - £30m = £70m, whereas if no oil is found a loss of £30m is made.

Step 2

Working from the right, the EMV at the chance nodes a, c and d are calculated as follows:

Node	EMV
a	$0.5 \times 70 + 0.5 \times (-30) = £20m$
c	$0.7 \times 65 + 0.3 \times (-35) = £35m$
d	$0.3 \times 65 + 0.7 \times (-35) = -£5m$

(The EMV at node b cannot be calculated until Step 3.)

The roll-back technique is now employed. At decision node 2, the decision is to either drill or sell. Sell will give you £30m, whereas drilling will give you £35m. The option that gives the largest EMV is to drill, and so this is the option that would be taken. The value 35 is put above node 2 and the sell option is crossed out. If you repeat this for node 3 you should find that the

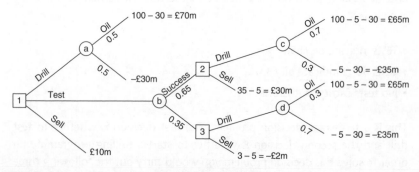

Figure 5.8 Decision tree for the Delma Oil company

best option here is to sell. The EMV at chance node b can now be calculated and you should find that this is £22.05m (0.65 × 35 + 0.35 × (−2)). You can now go to decision node 1 and compare the three decisions. You should find the following:

Drill: £20m
Test: £22.05m
Sell: £10m

The best decision is to test first. If the test gives successful results, only then should drilling start; otherwise the rights should be sold for £3m. You will see this analysis illustrated in Figure 5.9.

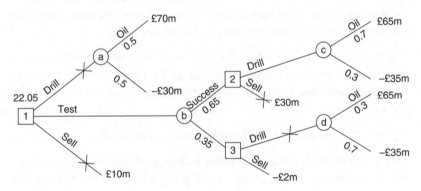

Figure 5.9 Completed decision tree for Delma Oil company

Decision trees and Bayes' theorem

In Example 5.3 you were given all the relevant probabilities, but in general you are more likely to be given just the prior probabilities and the conditional probabilities. You would then need to work out the relevant posterior probabilities using Bayes' theorem.

Example 5.4

A small motor component company, CleanFuel, is trying to decide whether to market a fuel additive which it claims will improve fuel consumption.

Unfortunately there are a number of competitors in the market who are also working on the same product and CleanFuel knows that if it decides to market the product it will face stiff competition from other companies.

Instead of marketing the product itself, it could sell the rights to it for £2m. However, if it goes ahead and markets the product itself, it estimates that the probability that sales will be high is only 0.2. The profit resulting from these high sales is put at £10m, but if the sales are low (with a probability of 0.8), the company will end up making a loss of £1m. An alternative is to commission a market research survey to see if motorists would purchase the product. This market research would indicate either high or low sales. From past experience CleanFuel knows that this particular market research company is better at predicting high rather than low sales. When sales have turned out to be high the company has been correct 75% of the time, but when sales have been low the company has only managed a 65% success rate.

The market research is confidential, so even if the results of the research indicate low sales it will still be possible to sell the rights for £2m. Of course, CleanFuel could also decide to market the product whatever the results of the survey.

Figure 5.10 is the decision tree for this particular problem.

Notice that there are some probabilities that we don't appear to know. These are the probability of the market research giving a high and low forecast and the probability of high and low demand given the different outcomes of the market research. These probabilities can be obtained by the use of Bayes' theorem. The prior probabilities are 0.2 for high sales and 0.8 for low sales. A probability tree can be used to help calculate these probabilities.

The probabilities at the end of the tree are the joint probabilities found by multiplying the two probabilities along that branch of the tree (e.g. $0.2 \times 0.75 = 0.15$).

We can now calculate the missing probabilities as follows:

P(market research indicates high sales) = 0.15 + 0.28 = 0.43

P(market research indicates low sales) = 1 – 0.43 = 0.57

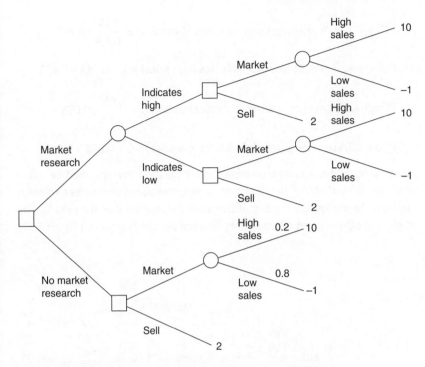

Figure 5.10 Decision tree for the CleanFuel problem (Example 5.4)

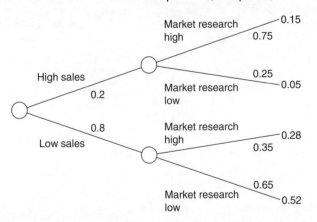

Figure 5.11 Probability tree diagram for the CleanFuel problem (Example 5.4)

P(high sales | market research indicates high sales) = $\frac{0.15}{0.43}$ = 0.349

P(low sales | market research indicates high sales) = 1 − 0.349 = 0.651

P(high sales | market research indicates low sales) = $\frac{0.05}{0.57}$ = 0.088

P(low sales | market research indicates low sales) = 1 − 0.088 = 0.912

These probabilities can now be added to the decision tree and the tree rolled back to show that the best decision is to commission the market research and only to market the product if the research suggests that the sales will be high, and otherwise to sell the rights. You can see the final tree in Figure 5.12.

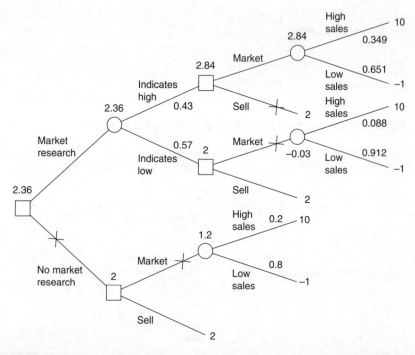

Figure 5.12 The completed decision tree for the CleanFuel problem (Example 5.4)

KEY POINTS

★ Probability is measured on a scale of 0 to 1.

★ When two or more events can happen at the same time, the addition rule can be used to calculate the probability of either of the events occurring.

★ When events occur in sequence, the multiplication rule is used.

★ Conditional probability is when the probability of an event occurring is dependent on whether another event has occurred.

★ Tree diagrams should be used for problems involving conditional probability.

★ When we want to update some prior probability with new information, Bayes' theorem is used.

★ Bayes' theorem allows the posterior probabilities to be calculated.

★ Expected value is a long-run average; that is, it is the average value you would get if you could repeat an experiment a large number of times. The term EMV is used when the outcomes are financial.

★ Decision trees are used in conjunction with probabilities to choose between a number of alternatives.

FURTHER READING

Probability is a wide subject and can be treated in many different ways. Students taking a maths or statistics degree would probably want a more mathematical text such as Swift and Piff (2010). A classic text is the one by Sheldon (2010). However this is only for students with a good background in mathematics. For those of you interested in sport and gambling there are a number of texts that show how probability can help improve your understanding of the issues involved. Examples are Haigh (2000) and Barboianu (2006). Haigh is a particularly easy-to-read text. A similar treatment to the one here is given in Chapters 6 and 11 of Oakshott (2012). There are also many resources that can help in your understanding of probability. The Plus magazine (http://plus.maths.org/content) is aimed at schools but will be of interest to university undergraduates too.

REVISION QUESTIONS

1 A bag contains 5 red discs, 3 yellow discs and 2 green discs.

   (a) A disc is picked from the bag. What is the probability that the disc will be:

   (i) red?

   (ii) yellow?

   (iii) not yellow?

   (b) Two discs are picked from the bag with replacement. What is the probability that the discs will be:

   (i) both red?

   (ii) 1 red and 1 yellow?

   (c) Repeat part (b) if the discs are picked without replacement.

2 Three machines – A, B and C – operate independently in a factory. Machine A is out of action for 10% of the time, while B is out of action 5% of the time and C is out of action for 20% of the time. A rush order has to be commenced at midday tomorrow. What is the probability that at this time:

   (a) All three of the machines will be out of action?

   (b) None of the machines will be out of action?

3 A light bulb is to be selected at random from a box of 100 bulbs, details of which are given below.

Type of bulb	Defective	Satisfactory
60 watts	20	40
100 watts	10	30

Find:

   (i) P(bulb is defective)

   (ii) P(bulb is defective | selected bulb is 60 watts)

4 Cast Iron Construction plc (CIC) is a company specializing in high-rise office blocks. They have recently decided to consider building in Third World countries and they have a choice of 2 sites. One is in the earthquake-prone island of Tutamolia and the other is in the politically unstable country of Flesomnial.

The building cost of £5m is the same for both countries, and it is estimated that that the return over 10 years for each country will also be the same at £20m. However, in Tutamolia, CIC have a choice of strengthening the building at a further cost of £5m. If they do this the probability that the building will collapse if an earthquake occurs is only 0.01, whereas if no strengthening work is done the probability that the building would collapse is 0.7.

The probability that an earthquake will occur in the next 10 years is put at 0.1. If an earthquake does occur any time during the 10 years and the building collapses, the company will forfeit the return of £20m, and in addition they will have to pay compensation to the government of £10m.

If CIC decides to build in Flesomnial there is a 20% chance that the country will be taken over by a dictator and the company will not receive any return on its investment.

Draw a decision tree for this problem and use this decision tree to determine the decision that will maximize CIC'c expected return.

5 A simple screening test can be conducted to indicate if someone has a particular medical condition or not. However, the test sometimes gives incorrect results.

A false positive result (when the person does not have the condition) occurs 5% of the time and a false negative result (when the person has the condition) occurs 10% of the time. It is estimated that 2% of the population have the condition. Draw a probability tree of the situation and mark on it all given probabilities.

What is the probability that a person tested at random will not have the condition given that they test positive and what is the probability that they will have the condition given they test negative?

6 Jayes Pharmaceutical has a number of high earning products, including the new A1 asthma spray. Preliminary sales of this product suggest that profits per unit sold amount to £10.

However, a recent report in an American journal suggests that A1 can cause an allergic reaction in up to 1% of people using the spray. The company now has a dilemma: should it continue selling the spray, knowing that there is this risk, or should it abandon it and re-market an older, less effective spray?

If it continues to sell this product and allergies develop, the company will have to compensate the buyer and the loss in profits will cost the company £20 per unit.

If the company decides to abandon the product and sell the older version, it would expect to earn a profit of £1.50 per unit.

An alternative is to supply a free allergy testing kit worth £1 with each product sold. If the test is positive, the customer will get a full refund. This test is not perfectly reliable, however: the probability that the test will correctly indicate that someone will be allergic is only 0.9 and the probability that it will give a false positive reading is 0.3. The company would not be able to recover the costs of supplying this kit, so the company would effectively make a loss of £11.

(a) Draw a probability tree diagram showing the prior and conditional probabilities.
(b) Calculate the probability that the test will be positive.
(c) Calculate the following posterior probabilities:
    (i) probability that a person is allergic if the test is positive
    (ii) probability that a person is allergic if the test is negative
(d) Draw a decision tree to determine the best course of action.
(e) If the company expected to sell 500 000 of these units per year, write down the annual profits from all three courses of action.

6

PROBABILITY DISTRIBUTIONS

OBJECTIVES

- To understand the difference between continuous and discrete probability distributions
- To be able to calculate binomial probabilities
- To be able to calculate Poisson probabilities
- To be able to use the Poisson distribution as an approximation to the binomial distribution
- To understand how the shape of the normal distribution is affected by the mean and standard deviation of the data
- To be able to use the normal distribution table
- To know how to use the normal distribution as an approximation to both the binomial and Poisson distributions

INTRODUCTION

This chapter examines some very important probability distributions. The *binomial distribution* is a discrete distribution, and is used when there are only two possible outcomes. The *Poisson distribution* is another discrete distribution, and is used for modelling rare events or events that occur at random. The final distribution you will meet is the *normal distribution*, and this (continuous) distribution has applications in almost all aspects of daily life, such as deciding whether the weight of a loaf of bread is outside acceptable limits or whether a child's height or weight is abnormal in some way.

Earnings distribution in the UK

The distribution of earnings in the UK is *right* (or *positively*) skewed (see Figure 6.1). This means that the vast majority of taxpayers are earning modest salaries, while a relatively few people are earning a considerably more. Table 6.1 gives some statistics from 2010–2011

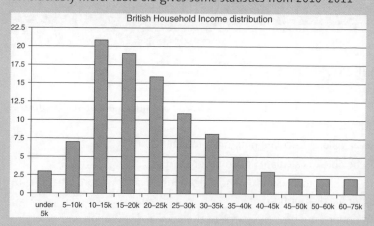

Figure 6.1 Distribution of net income (after tax)

Source: From http://en.wikipedia.org/wiki/Income_in_the_United_Kingdom, reused under the terms of Creative Commons, http://creativecommons.org/licenses/by-sa/3.0/

Table 6.1   Gross earnings 2010–2011

Statistic	Income before tax
Mean	£27,400
Median	£19,500
25% earn less than	£12,700
26% earn more than	£27,300

Source: HM Revenue and Customs

The fact that the mean is much higher than the median confirms the skewness of the distribution. This is reinforced by the fact only 26% of taxpayers earn more than the mean.

DISCRETE AND CONTINUOUS PROBABILITY DISTRIBUTIONS

The differences between discrete and continuous data were discussed in Chapter 2, but essentially discrete data is obtained by counting, whereas continuous data is obtained by measurement. So counting the number of loaves of bread baked over a period of time would give you data that only contained whole numbers, while recording the weight of each loaf of bread baked would give you data that could take on any value.

Example 6.1

Data on the number and weight of a 'standard' loaf of bread were collected over a period of time and aggregated into Table 6.2.

In order to compare the two data sets in more detail, diagrams could be used. A bar chart would be appropriate for the number of loaves baked, while a histogram is necessary for the weight data. These diagrams are shown in Figures 6.2 and 6.3.

Table 6.2 Frequency table for the data on the number and weight of loaves of bread

Number of loaves baked		Weight of each loaf	
Number	Frequency	Weight range	Frequency
20	8	770g to below 775g	3
21	12	775g to below 780g	17
22	24	780g to below 785g	44
23	26	785g to below 790g	100
24	35	790g to below 795g	141
25	35	795g to below 800g	192
26	30	800g to below 805g	191
27	28	805g to below 810g	150
28	21	810g to below 815g	90
		815g to below 820g	42
		820g to below 825g	14
		825g to below 830g	9

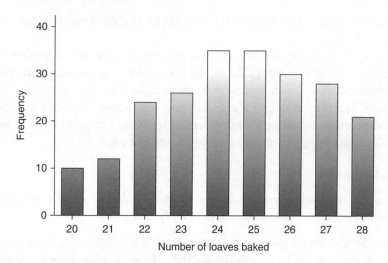

Figure 6.2 Bar chart for the number of loaves baked

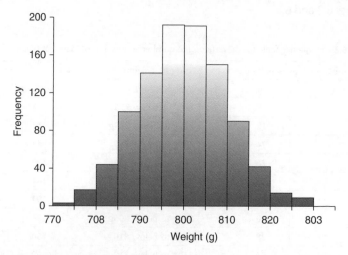

Figure 6.3 Histogram for the weight of a loaf

The histogram gives you an idea of the underlying distribution of the data; that is, it shows you how the data is distributed across the range of possible values. This kind of distribution is called an empirical distribution because it is obtained by measurement or observation. There are also distributions that can be derived mathematically. The three most common distributions are the binomial distribution, the Poisson distribution and the normal distribution.

The binomial distribution

This is a discrete probability distribution and arises when:

• A variable can only be in one of two states (an either/or situation).

• The probability of the two outcomes are known and constant from trial to trial.

• The number of trials is known and constant.

• Successive events are independent.

An easy example to use here is a coin since it can be in one of two states, either a head (H) or a tail (T) with a 50% chance of either. If you tossed a coin three times then the possible outcomes are:

HHH, HHT, HTH, HTT, THH, TTH, TTT

This is shown in the tree diagram below:

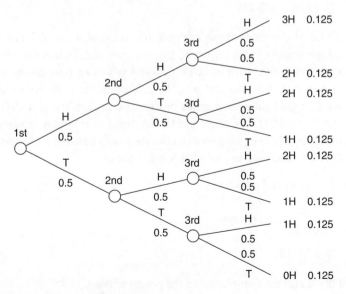

Figure 6.4 A coin tossed three times

From this diagram you could work out the probability of any number of heads. For example the probability of exactly 2 heads is $3 \times 0.125 = 0.375$, since 2 heads occurs 3 times. We call the number of tosses the number of *trials* and the number of heads the desired *outcome* (the 'success').

Instead of using a tree diagram to work out these types of problems you can use the binomial distribution for finding the probability ($P(r)$) of r successes. The formula is:

$$P(r) = {}^nC_r p^r (1-p)^{n-r}$$

where n is the number of trials, r the number of successes, p is the probability of a success and ${}^nC_r = \dfrac{n!}{r!(n-r)!}$ and is the number of ways of choosing r items from n. So if we tossed a coin 3 times ($n = 3$) then the number of ways of getting 2 heads ($r = 2$) is $\dfrac{3!}{2!1!} = 3$.

The probability of getting exactly 2 heads using the formula is

$$3 \times (0.5)^2(0.5) = 0.375$$

In the case of the coin-tossing example the value of p was 0.5 as a head and tail are equally likely. However, the binomial distribution can be used in many applications, such as quality control where an item can be either defective or not defective and p is likely to be quite small. For example, suppose in a particular production process the probability of a defective item is 3% (or 0.03). We could use the binomial distribution to work out the probability of say getting no defective items in a batch of 20. In this case $p = .03$, $n = 20$ and $r = 0$ so using the formula we get

$$P(0) = {}^{20}C_0 \times 0.03^0 \times (1-0.03)^{20}$$

$$= \frac{20!}{0! \times 20!} \times 1 \times 0.5438$$

$$= 0.54379$$

(Note $0! = 1$ and anything raised to the power of 0 is 1.)

We could also work out the probability of say getting 2 or more defective items. However rather than work out the probability of 2, 3, 4, and so on, an easier way is to work out the probability of 0 and 1 defective items and subtract the sum of these from 1. So

$P(r \geq 2) = 1 - (P(0) + P(1))$

$P(1) = \dfrac{20!}{1! \times 19!} \times 0.03^1 \times 0.97^{19}$

$= 20 \times 0.03 \times 0.56061$

$= 0.3364$

So $P(r \geq 2) = 1 - (0.54379 + 0.3364)$

$= 0.1198$

You can also use Excel to calculate binomial probabilities. The function name is

```
= BINOMDIST(number_s, trials, probability_s,
Cumulative)
```

where number_s is the number of successes in trials [that is, r]; trials is the number of independent trials [that is, n]; probability_s is the probability of success on each trial [that is, p]. Cumulative is a logical value that determines the form of the function. If Cumulative is true, then BINOMDIST returns the cumulative distribution function, which is the probability that there are at most number_s successes; if false, it returns the probability mass function, which is the probability that there are number_s successes.

(Taken from the Help facility in Excel.)

In our example the function to give 1 or less defective items would be

==BINOMDIST(1,20,0.03, TRUE)

which gives a value of 0.8802

So $P(r \geq 2) = 1 - 0.8802)$

$= 0.1198$

which agrees with the probability calculated earlier.

Properties of the binomial distribution

The shape of the binomial distribution depends on the value of r and n. When these two values are small the distribution is right-skewed; when n is large and r is close to 0.5 the distribution tends to be symmetrical.

The mean of a binomial distribution is np

The standard deviation is given by the formula

$$\sigma = \sqrt{np(1-p)}$$

The Poisson distribution

The Poisson distribution is another example of a discrete probability distribution and arises when:

• A variable can be in one of two possible states.
• The mean number of successes is known and constant.
• The probability of success is small (the event is 'rare').

The Poisson distribution is often used in situations where the event is unlikely (accidents, machine failures) or where the event occurs at random (arrivals of calls at a switchboard, for example).

The formula for the Poisson is less complicated than the binomial, and the probability of r events in a given unit (of time or length, and so on) is as follows:

$$P(r) = \frac{e^{-m}m^r}{r!}$$

where m is the mean number of events in the same unit and e is the constant 2.7182818 ... and can be found on many scientific calculators (usually in the form e^x).

A typical example of the Poisson distribution is as follows. The number of calls to a switchboard is random, with a mean of 1.5 per minute. What is the probability that there are no calls in any one minute?

All we need to do is to substitute $r = 0$ and $m = 1.5$ into the equation. That is:

$$P(0) = \frac{e^{-1.5}(1.5)^0}{0!}$$

$$= \frac{0.2231 \times 1}{1} = 0.2231$$

As in the case of the binomial distribution we can use the fact that the sum of the probabilities must be 1, so if we say we wanted the probability of more than 2 calls in a minute we simply find the probability of 0, 1 and 2 calls and subtract the sum from 1.

As with the binomial distribution we can also use Excel to calculate the probabilities. The function is = `Poisson(x, mean, cumulative)`

x is the number of events (that is r)

mean is the expected numeric value (that is m)

cumulative is a logical value as before (True for cumulative probability from 0 to x)

The Poisson can in some circumstances be used instead of the binomial distribution. The conditions for this approximation to be valid are:

- The number of trials, n, is large (greater than 30)
- The probability of a success, p, is small (less than 0.1).
- The mean number of successes, $n \times p$, is less than 5.

To demonstrate this approximation we could try the quality control example we looked at earlier. In this case $n = 20$, $p = 0.03$ so $m = 20 \times .03 = 0.6$.

$$P(0) = \frac{e^{-0.6}}{0!}$$

$$= 0.5488$$

The actual value was 0.5438 which is a difference of less than a 1%. This is quite good considering that the conditions were not quite met.

Properties of the Poisson distribution

The Poisson distribution has a 'memoryless' property. This means that events are independent and are not affected by previous events. It is very good at modelling arrivals to a queue.

It also is related to the negative exponential distribution (a continuous distribution), so if you know the mean number of arrivals in a fixed unit of time you know the time between arrivals and vice versa.

The shape of the Poisson distribution depends on the mean value. For low values of m (that is for rare events) the distribution is right-skewed, but as the mean increases the distribution becomes more symmetrical. The standard deviation of the Poisson distribution is the square root of the mean. That is

$$\sigma = \sqrt{m}$$

The normal distribution

Many observations that are obtained from measurements follow the normal distribution. For example, the heights of people and the weights of loaves of bread are approximately normally distributed. The normal distribution is completely symmetrical or bell shaped. The mean, mode and median of this distribution all lie at the centre of the bell, as you can see in Figure 6.5

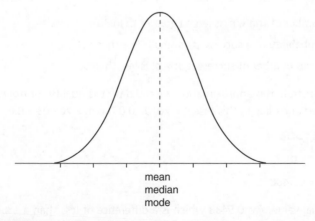

mean
median
mode

Figure 6.5 The normal distribution

The normal curve has the following properties:

1. The curve is symmetrical about the mean.

2. The total area under the curve is equal to 1 or 100%.

3. The horizontal axis represents a continuous variable such as weight.

4. The area under the curve between two points on the horizontal axis represents the probability that the value of the variable lies between these two points.

5. The position and shape of the curve depends on the mean and standard deviation of the distribution. As the standard deviation gets larger, the curve will get flatter and extend further on either side of the mean.

The standard normal distribution

The standard normal distribution has a mean of zero and a standard deviation of 1. This is illustrated in Figure 6.6. The figures along the horizontal axis are the number of standard deviations and are called the Z values.

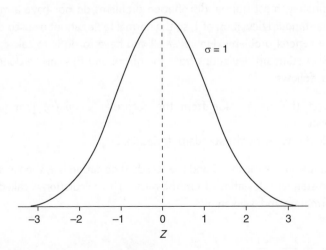

Figure 6.6 The standard normal distibution

To demonstrate the use of the normal table you should now refer to the table provided in Appendix 1. The table provided in this book gives you the area in the right-hand tail of the distribution. The first column gives the Z value to one decimal place and the first row gives the second place of decimals. For example, for a Z value of 0.55, you should have found a value of 0.2912 or 29.12%. This is the area in the tail for Z being greater than 0.55. Since the distribution is symmetrical, the area being less than Z = –0:55 is also 29.12%. You can also deduce that the area less than Z = 0.55 is 1 – .2912 = 0.7088 or 70.88%. The area between Z = 0 and Z = 0.55 will be 0.5 – .2912 = 0.2088 or 20.88%. To find an area say from Z = 0.55 to Z = 1 you find the areas greater than the two values of Z and subtract the smaller from the larger. So for Z = 1 the area is 0.1587 and the difference in area will be 0.2912–0.1587 = 0.1325 or 13.25%.

You can also use the table in reverse. So if you wanted to know the value of Z equivalent to the 5% upper tail, you would need to find an area of 0.05. Looking in the tables you will see that a Z value of 1.64 gives an area of 0.0505 and Z=1.65 gives an area of 0.0495. Either would be acceptable or to get a more accurate figure you could take the average of these two values which is 1.645

Standardizing normal distributions

Unfortunately, most normal distribution problems do not have a mean of zero or a standard deviation of 1, so the normal table cannot be used directly to solve general problems. However, all you have to do is to calculate the number of standard deviations from the mean, and this can be done quite easily, as follows:

- Subtract the mean value from the particular value (x) that you are interested in.
- Divide this value by the standard deviation.

For example, if the mean is 5 and the standard deviation is 2, then a value of 9 is two standard deviations from the mean. This calculation is called the Z transformation and is given by:

$$Z = \frac{x - \text{mean}}{\text{standard deviation}}$$

For example suppose a batch of loaves is baked. The weight of the loaves is normally distributed with a mean of 800 g and a standard deviation of 10 g. What proportion of loaves will weigh more than 815 g?

Substituting these values into the equation gives:

$$Z = \frac{815 - 800}{10} = 1.5$$

That is 815 g is 1.5 standard deviations away from the mean. It is now a simple matter of looking up Z = 1.5 in the normal table. If you do this you should get an area of 0.0668 or 6.68%, which means that 6.68% of all loaves weigh more than 815 g. This is represented in Figure 6.7.

This calculation can be done for any value of x. If you need to find the area between two values of x you do each value separately as was done for the standard normal examples. However, if you wanted to ensure that no more than 5% of loaves are less than a certain weight, a little bit of algebra is required. The problem is shown in Figure 6.8 and you can see that the unknown in this case is the weight x. The value of Z for an area of 5% is

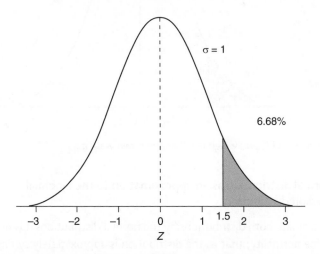

Figure 6.7 Proportion of loaves that weigh more than 815 g

1.645 as we found earlier. As the value is left of the mean this value of Z will be negative; that is, −1.645. Substituting this value into the formula gives:

$$-1.645 = \frac{x - 800}{10} - 16.45 = x - 800$$

$x = 800 - 16.45 = 783.6$ g

So no more than 5% of loaves should weigh less than 783.6 g

To become proficient at solving normal distribution problems, it is suggested that you attempt lots of different problems. There are several questions for you to tackle in the revision questions at the end of this chapter. Whenever you need to solve normal distribution problems it is advised that you always draw a diagram first.

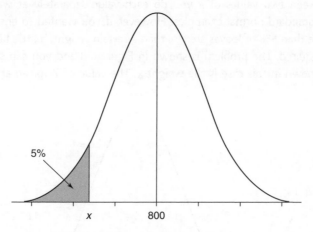

Figure 6.8 5% of loaves weigh less than unknown weight x

The normal distribution as an approximation to the binomial and Poisson distributions

To approximate both distributions by the normal distributions it is necessary to assume normality; that is, the distribution is approximately symmetrical. For the binomial distribution this occurs when $n \times p$ and $n \times (1 - p)$ are greater than 5. For the Poisson distribution the value of m needs to be greater than 10. We also need to find the mean and standard deviation of the equivalent normal distribution using the appropriate formulae. Finally we have to make a *continuity correction*. This is because the binomial and Poisson distributions are discrete probability distributions, whereas the normal distribution is a continuous one. So if we were trying to find the probability of say 5 successes we would need to assume that the discrete value 5 is a continuous variable in the range 4.5 to 5.5.

KEY POINTS

★ Distributions can be either discrete or continuous.

★ Examples of discrete distributions include the binomial distribution and the Poisson distribution.

★ The binomial distribution is used when an event can either happen or not happen. The Poisson distribution is used when the chance of an event happening is very small (it is a rare event). It is used where events occur at random such as arrivals to a queue.

★ The normal distribution is a continuous distribution and is the most widely used distribution in statistics. Before a normal distribution problem can be solved it needs to be transformed into the standard normal form which has a mean of zero and a standard deviation of 1. Tables are used to find the area (and therefore probability) of part of the distribution of interest.

★ It is often possible to approximate the binomial and Poisson distributions by the normal distribution as it is easier to find probabilities for this distribution.

FURTHER READING

Like probability there are a large number of texts on probability distributions, ranging from introductory level to more advanced texts. Chapter 7 of Oakshott (2012) gives a similar treatment to this text as does Curwin and Slater (2008). Morris (2012) gives a good general description of the common distributions (binomial, Poisson and normal) without using many equations.

REVISION QUESTIONS

1 The sex ratio of newborn infants is about 105 males to 100 females. If 4 infants are chosen at random, what is the probability that:
- (a) All four are males.
- (b) Exactly three are male.
- (c) Two are male and two are female.

2 Calls arrive at a switchboard according to the Poisson distribution. If the average number of calls received in a 5-minute period is 6.7, find the probability that:
- (a) There are fewer than 4 calls received in a 5-minute period.
- (b) There are more than 7 calls received during a 5-minute period.
- (c) There are no calls received in a 1-minute period.

3 A particular normal distribution has a mean of 5 and a standard deviation of 1.5.
What is the area corresponding to a value:
- (a) greater than 6?
- (b) less than 4?
- (c) between 4 and 6?
- (d) between 6.5 and 7.5?

4 A recent large survey found that the average annual salary in the food industry was £45,121 with a standard deviation of £24,246. If an employee is chosen at random what is the probability that he will earn more than £80,000? If there are 500,000 people working in the banking industry how many of them will earn more than £100,000?

5 Crumbly Biscuits produces golden cream biscuits which are sold in notional 300 g packets. The weights of these packets are normally distributed with a mean of 320 g and a standard deviation of 10.4 g.

(a) What is the probability that if you select a packet at random it will weigh:
   (i) less than 300 g?
   (ii) more than 325 g?
   (iii) between 318 and 325 g?
(b) Out of a batch of 500 packets, how many would weigh less than 300 g?
(c) It has been decided to reduce the mean weight to 310 g. What would the standard deviation need to be if no more than 3% of packets must weigh less than 300 g?

7

ANALYSIS OF SAMPLE DATA

OBJECTIVES

- To be able to calculate best estimates of the mean and standard deviation of a population
- To be able to calculate confidence intervals for a population mean
- To be able to calculate confidence intervals for a population percentage

INTRODUCTION

You were introduced to the idea of sampling in Chapter 1, where the problems of recording information about the whole 'population' were discussed and the need for sampling became apparent. Information from a sample is subject to error, and the purpose of this chapter is to be able to *quantify* this error. This is achieved by stating the margin of error that accompanies the sample estimate of a given population parameter. Thus it is possible to calculate the margin of error for opinion polls for example.

Statistical Confidence Intervals for the Bank of Canada's Business Outlook Survey

Since 1997 The Bank of Canada has carried out a quarterly Business Outlook Survey (BOS). This survey obtains factual information on such things as business activity, prices and credit, but it also obtains opinions on outlook for sales, growth, employment, etc. Quota sampling is used to select 100 firms from which this information is obtained. As the sample is therefore non-random the usual methods of obtaining confidence around its results is not valid. Since the results of the survey feed into the monetary policy decision-making process, the importance of accuracy is paramount.

Work done in 2009[1] indicated that the sampling approach used did not result in significantly biased estimates or wider confidence intervals than if a random sample had been used. More recent research by Daniel de Munnik has shown that confidence intervals around population proportions (for example, those with Yes/No responses) are about half those for the questions involving subjective opinions (such as positive/No change/Negative). They also found that the width of the confidence intervals for these types of questions can change from survey to survey.

Source: Daniel de Munnik; May 2010 – Bank of Canada Discussion paper

SAMPLES AND SAMPLING

We often think of sampling as a survey of consumer's opinion as we often get requests from organizations to take part in a survey on their product or services. However, sampling people's views and intentions is notoriously difficult and even the best sampling plan can fail in these circumstances. Fortunately, when sampling is done by measurement, the results tend to be much more reliable. Sampling in industry and business tends to be of the measurement kind, and it will be this aspect of sampling that will be emphasized here.

Whenever we take samples we must ensure that the samples are selected at random; that is, every member of the population must have an equal chance of being selected (See Chapter 1). This means we must use a probabilistic sampling method such as simple random sampling and a *sampling frame* (a list of the population) must be available.

POINT ESTIMATES

The whole purpose of obtaining a sample from a population is to obtain estimates of various population parameters, such as the mean, the standard deviation or percentage.

These parameters can also be obtained for the sample, and it is the purpose of this section to show how the population parameters and the sample statistics are related. However, before continuing, it is necessary to define the symbols that are to be used throughout this (and the next) chapter.

The convention is to use Greek letters for the population parameters and normal letters for the sample statistics. The various symbols used are given below.

Parameter	Population	Sample
Mean	μ	$\bar{x}$
Standard deviation	σ	s
Percentage	π	P

The one exception to this rule is that the size of the population is usually referred to as N and the sample size as n.

SAMPLING DISTRIBUTION OF THE MEAN

Imagine that you took lots and lots of samples and calculated the mean of each. Each mean is an estimate of the population value, and therefore the 'mean of the means' should be an even better estimate. If you then plotted the distribution of the means, what shape would you expect the distribution to be? The answer is that the shape would tend towards the normal curve. The degree of agreement with the normal curve depends on two factors:

• the distribution of the population values
• the sample size

If the population values are normally distributed, the 'sampling distribution of the means' would also be normal. If the population is not normally distributed, the agreement with the normal distribution depends on the sample size; the larger the sample size, the closer the agreement. This very important result is known as the *central limit theorem*.

In addition, the spread of this sampling distribution depends on the sample size; the larger the sample size, the smaller the spread (that is, the standard deviation). The standard deviation of the sampling distribution is called the *standard error*, as it measures the error that could arise in your estimate due to the spread of the sampling distribution. To avoid confusion with the standard error of the sampling distribution of a percentage, which will be discussed later, the standard error of the sampling distribution of the means will be referred to as STEM (the STandard Error of the Mean). Is it necessary to collect many samples in order to calculate the value of STEM? Fortunately not, as there is a relationship between σ and STEM. This relationship is as follows:

$$\text{STEM} = \frac{\sigma}{\sqrt{n}}$$

So the larger the sample size (n), the smaller the value of STEM, which makes sense.

These ideas are illustrated in Figure 7.1. Two sampling distributions are shown: one for a sample size of 4, and one for a sample size of 16. The population distribution (assumed normal in this case) has been superimposed on to the diagram.

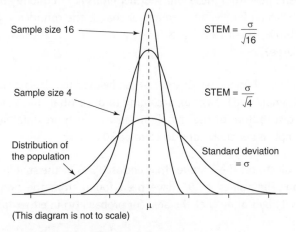

(This diagram is not to scale)

Figure 7.1 Sampling distribution of the means

You will see that the mean of each sampling distribution is the same and equal to the population value. You would normally only take one sample, and from Figure 7.1 you can see that the mean of a sample can lie anywhere within the relevant sampling distribution, although it is more likely to be near the centre than in the tails. This variation depends on the value of STEM, so the smaller this figure, the more reliable your estimate of the population mean will be.

CONFIDENCE INTERVALS FOR A POPULATION MEAN FOR LARGE SAMPLES

Rather than simply quote the value of STEM, a much better idea of the reliability of your estimate is to specify some limits within which the true mean is expected to lie. These limits are called *confidence limits* or *confidence intervals*.

When calculating confidence intervals it is necessary to decide what level of confidence you wish to use. The most common level is 95%, which means that you are 95% confident that the true mean lies within the calculated limits. Or, put another way, there is a 5% chance that the true mean doesn't lie within these limits. Other limits are frequently used, such as 90%, 99% and 99.9%, but remember that as the confidence level gets closer to 100%, the interval gets larger and larger (at 100% it would be infinitely large).

The normal distribution (see Chapter 6) can be used to calculate these limits when the sample size is large as, according to the central limit theorem, the sampling distribution of the sample mean will be approximately normal. A large sample is generally considered to be 30 or over.

Figure 7.2 illustrates the Z values that enclose 95% of the standard normal distribution. The values ±1.96 have been found from the normal table (Appendix 1) by noting that the area (or probability) in either tail is 0.025 (= 0.05/2).

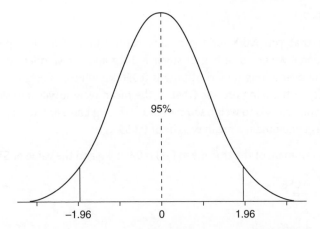

Figure 7.2 95% confidence interval for the standard normal distribution

From the previous chapter, you will know that any normal distribution can be transformed into the standard normal distribution using the formula:

$$Z = \frac{x - \mu}{\sigma}$$

However, this formula is for individual x values. For a sampling distribution of the means, the x needs to be replaced by $\bar{x}$ and σ needs to be replaced by STEM. The formula then becomes:

$$Z = \frac{\bar{x} - \mu}{STEM}$$

If you rearrange this equation to make μ the subject you will get:

$$\mu = \bar{x} \pm Z \times STEM$$

This is the equation you would use to calculate confidence intervals using the normal distribution. For 95% confidence intervals, the Z value is 1.96 and the formula becomes:

$$\mu = \bar{x} \pm 1.96 \times STEM$$

Example 7.1

Imagine that you work for the quality control unit of a sugar producer. The notional weight of a bag of sugar is 1 kg and the standard deviation measured over a long period of time is 0.056 kg which reflects the natural variability in the filing process (that is, the mean weight will vary slightly). One of your tasks is to weigh samples of these 1 kg bags, and from a sample of 36 bags you obtain a mean weight of 0.985 kg.

The best estimate of the true mean (μ) is 0.985 kg and the value of STEM is:

$$\frac{\sigma}{\sqrt{n}} = \frac{0.056}{\sqrt{36}}$$

$$= 0.00933$$

Therefore the 95% confidence interval for the true mean is:

$$0.985 \pm 1.96 \times 0.00933$$

$$= 0.985 - 0.018 \text{ and } 0.985 + 0.018$$

$$= 0.967 \text{ and } 1.003 \text{ kg}$$

The 0.967 kg is the lower limit and 1.003 kg is the upper limit. The ±0.018 is often called the *half width* of the confidence interval. It is usual to write this confidence interval as:

0.967, 1.003 kg or 0.967 to 1.003 kg

This interval tells us that we are 95% confident that the true mean is between the two limits. (As this interval straddles 1 kg it appears that the machine is functioning normally but more about statistical tests in the next chapter.)

CONFIDENCE INTERVALS FOR A POPULATION MEAN FOR SMALL SAMPLES

When we take a sample we often do not know the standard deviation of the population and have to estimate it from the sample. This doesn't matter for large samples as the standard deviation of the sample should be close to the population value. For large samples we can also assume that the sampling distribution of the mean will be normal no matter the shape of the distribution of the population. However for small samples both these issues can introduce errors. To compensate for these problems a different distribution is used, called the 't-distribution'. This distribution is symmetrical like the normal, but it is flatter. This 'flatness' increases the percentage of the distribution in the 'tails' and this means that the confidence interval, for the same confidence level, is wider. The amount of 'flatness' decreases with increase in n, the sample size. When n is 50 there is virtually no difference between the two distributions, and even for a sample size of 30 the difference is quite small.

Figure 7.3 shows the t-distribution for a sample size of 6, together with the normal distribution for comparison.

The t-table is given in Appendix 1. If you compare this table with the normal table, you will see two important differences. First, the numbers within the table are t-values and not probabilities; second, the numbers in the first column are different. These numbers are the degrees of freedom (v) of the sample. Degrees of freedom can be thought of as the 'freedom' that you have in choosing the values of the sample. If you were given the mean of the sample of 6 values, you would be free to choose 5 of the 6 but not the sixth one. Therefore there are 5 degrees of freedom. The number of degrees of freedom for a single sample of size n is $n - 1$. For a very large sample

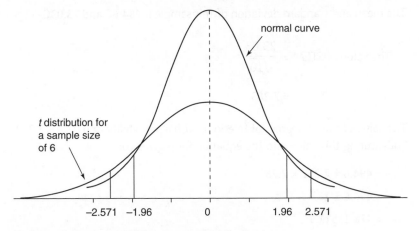

Figure 7.3 Comparison of the normal and t-distributions

(shown as ∞ in the table) the t and Z distributions are exactly the same. To use this table you would first decide on the probability level. For a 95% confidence interval you would choose the 0.025 level, since this represents 2.5% in each tail. For a sample size of 6, the degrees of freedom is 5, so the t-value for 5 degrees of freedom at 95% confidence level is 2.571. This value has been shown in Figure 7.3. (Remember that the t-distribution is symmetrical about the mean of zero, so the equivalent value in the left-hand side of the distribution is –2.571.)

The formula for calculating confidence intervals using this distribution is the same as when the normal distribution was used, except that Z is replaced by t, and is therefore:

$$\mu = \bar{x} \pm t \times STEM$$

Example 7.2

It is required to find the 95% confidence interval for the true mean combustion temperature of plastic granules. Ten samples of granules were tested and the combustion temperatures (in deg C) are as follows:

Sample no.	1	2	3	4	5	6	7	8	9	10
Temperature	510	535	498	450	491	505	487	500	501	469

The mean and standard deviation of this sample is 494.6C and 23.03C.

$$\text{The value of STEM} = \frac{23.03}{\sqrt{10}}$$

$$= 7.283$$

The value of t for 9 degrees of freedom, with a probability of 0.025, is 2.262. Substituting this value into the equation for μ gives you:

$$\mu = 494.6 \pm 2.262 \times 7.283$$

$$= 494.6 \pm 16.6$$

$$= 478.1, 511.1$$

So the true mean combustion temperature of the whole consignment lies between 478.1C and 511.1C at the 95% level of confidence.

CONFIDENCE INTERVAL OF A PERCENTAGE

Percentages occur quite frequently in the analysis of survey results; for example, the percentage of people who like a particular product or the percentage of students over the age of 25. Provided n is large and the percentage is not too small or too large, the sampling distribution of a percentage can be approximated by the normal distribution.

The standard error of the sampling distribution of percentages (STEP) is:

$$STEP = \sqrt{\frac{P(100 - P)}{n}}$$

where P is the sample percentage.

The calculation of a confidence interval for a percentage is similar to that of the mean, that is:

$$\pi = P \pm Z \times STEP$$

So if you took a sample of 250 students and found that 147 were female, you could find the 95% confidence interval for the true percentage of female students as follows:

$$P = \frac{147}{250} \times 100$$

$$= 58.8\%$$

$$STEP = \sqrt{\frac{58.8 \times (100 - 58.8)}{250}}$$

$$= 3.113$$

The value of Z for 95% confidence is 1.96, so the confidence interval becomes:

$$\pi = 58.8 \pm 1.96 \times 3.113$$
$$= 58.8 \pm 6.1$$
$$= 52.7, 64.9$$

That is, the true percentage lies somewhere between 52.7% and 64.9%

CALCULATION OF SAMPLE SIZE

Since the value of both STEM and STEP depend on the sample size, the width of the confidence interval for the same confidence level can be reduced by increasing the value of n. For the sugar example (Example 7.2) the half width of the interval – that is, the difference between the lower or upper limit and the sample mean – is 0.018 kg for a confidence level of 95%. This was obtained by multiplying STEM by 1.96; that is:

Half width of confidence interval = $1.96 \times$ STEM

$$= 1.96 \times \frac{\sigma}{\sqrt{n}}$$

If you wanted to reduce this half width to, say, 0.015 kg, then you would need to calculate the value of n required to achieve this reduction. That is:

$$1.96 \times \frac{0.056}{\sqrt{n}} = 0.015$$

Rearranging this equation gives

$$\sqrt{n} = \frac{1.96 \times 0.056}{0.015}$$
$$= 7.3173$$

So $n = 53.5$

So a sample size of about 54 would be required to achieve an accuracy of ± 0.015 kg.

A similar process can be applied to percentage. So if we wanted to reduce the half width of the female student percentage from 6.1% to 1%, we would proceed as follows:

$$1.96 \times \text{STEP} = 1.0$$

$$1.96 \times \frac{58.8 \times (100 - 58.8)}{n} = 1$$

$$n = \frac{58.8 \times 41.2}{0.2603}$$

$$= 9306.8$$

That is, a sample of about 9000 students would need to be selected to ensure this level of accuracy!

KEY POINTS

★ A sample can be used to provide estimates of population parameters such as the mean, proportion and standard deviation.

★ Every estimate of these parameters will have a sampling error associated with them. We can reduce this error by taking a larger sample, but we can never eliminate the error entirely.

★ The central limit theorem allows us to calculate this error because we can assume that the sample mean (or proportion) comes from a normal distribution.

★ We normally express this error in the form of a confidence interval. The confidence is expressed in percentages and the common values are 95% and 99%.

★ We can calculate the sample size required to give a specific minimum error.

★ For small samples we use the t-distribution because for the same confidence level we get a slightly wider interval.

FURTHER READING

All statistical texts and many quantitative methods texts will have a chapter on confidence intervals. Texts aimed at the business student will treat the material in a similar way to this text, while those texts aimed at maths or stats students will be much more mathematical and probably beyond the ability of most business students. Morris (2012) is very descriptive and uses few equations apart for STEM and STEP. Chapter 8 in Oakshott (2012) uses a similar approach to the one used here.

REVISION QUESTIONS

1 A random sample of 100 adult females from the population of a large town has a mean height of 169.5 cm with a standard deviation of 2.6 cm. Construct a 95% confidence interval for the mean height of all adult females in the town.

2 A sample of 60 people was asked if they thought that if children watched video 'nasties' they were more likely to commit a crime. Out of the sample, 45 thought that they would. Calculate the 95% confidence interval for the true percentage.

3 The weight of each of 10 specimens of carbon paper was found to be (in grams):

7.4, 8.3, 10.9, 6.9, 7.9, 8.2, 8.6, 9.1, 9.9, 10.0

Given that the weights are normally distributed, construct (a) 95% and (b) 99% confidence intervals for the true mean of the population weights.

4 A credit card company wants to determine the mean income of its card holders.
A random sample of 225 card holders was drawn and the sample average income was £16 450 with a standard deviation of £3675.
(a) Construct a 99% confidence interval for the true mean income.
(b) Management decided that the confidence interval in (a) was too large to be useful. In particular, the management wanted to estimate

the mean income to within £200, with a confidence level of 99%. How large a sample should be selected?

5 A company wants to estimate, with 95% confidence, the percentage of people in a town who have seen its press advertisements. The company would like its estimate to have a margin of error of ±4%. How large a sample of people will they need to take if:
  (a) a preliminary estimate suggests that the true percentage is about 10%?
  (b) no preliminary estimate is available?

NOTE

1. de Munnik, D., D. Dupuis and M. Illing. 2009. 'Computing the Accuracy of Complex Non-Random Sampling Methods: The Case of the Bank of Canada's Business Outlook Survey'. Bank of Canada Working Paper No. 2009–2010.

8
HYPOTHESIS TESTING

OBJECTIVES

- To understand the ideas behind hypothesis testing
- To know how to perform tests of hypothesis on the mean of a population
- To know how to perform tests of hypothesis on a percentage
- To know how to perform a 'goodness-of-fit' test
- To be able to apply the chi-square test to categorical data

INTRODUCTION

In Chapter 7 you saw how to analyse a sample so that estimates of some population parameters, such as the mean or percentage, could be obtained. In this chapter the emphasis is slightly different in that you are told the value of the population parameter and then to find out whether or not a particular sample with this parameter could have come from this population.

Use of Business Analytics in Helping HMRC to Tackle Fraud

The definition of business analytics is 'the combination of skills, technologies, applications and processes used by organizations to gain insight into their business based on data and statistics to drive business planning. Business analytics is used to evaluate organization-wide operations, and can be implemented in any department from sales to product development to customer service' (www.webopedia.com).

With help from Capgemini, HMRC developed the Connect IT system that analysed millions of data items to identify high-risk sectors, companies and individuals. Statistical analyses were carried out on samples of data and results passed onto caseworkers to allow more specific investigation. The trial version of Connect helped increase the number of successful investigations which gave HMRC over £1.3 billion additional revenue. It is hoped that by 2014/5 the increase in revenue will amount to £7 billion.

Source: Capgemini UK

THE PURPOSE OF HYPOTHESIS TESTING

In Chapter 7 we took an example (Example 7.1) of a sugar producer where the mean weight was expected to be 1 kg with a standard deviation of 0.056 kg. The mean weight of a sample of 36 bags was found to be 0.985 kg. We found that the 95% confidence interval for the true mean weight was between 0.967 and 1.003 kg. As this range straddles 1 kg it looks as if the sample mean is consistent with the notional weight of 1 kg.

However, rather than use confidence intervals we can carry out a *hypothesis* test (or test of *significance*). This approach makes the hypothesis that any departure from the supposedly true mean by the sample mean is simply due to chance effects. It is then a matter of calculating the probability that this sample result could have occurred by chance. This is the general idea of hypothesis testing – it assumes that the hypothesis is true and then tries to disprove it. This hypothesis is known as the *null* hypothesis. If the null hypothesis is rejected, an *alternative* hypothesis is accepted. The null hypothesis is called H_0 and the alternative hypothesis H_1.

The null hypothesis is tested at a particular *significance* level. This level relates to the area (or probability) in the tail of the distribution being used for the test. This area is called the *critical region*, and if the test statistic lies in the critical region, you would infer that the result is unlikely to have occurred by chance. You would then reject the null hypothesis. For example, if the 5% level of significance was used and the null hypothesis was rejected, you would say that H_0 had been rejected at the 5% (or the 0.05) significance level, and the result was *significant*.

These ideas apply to all types of hypothesis tests. The precise form of each hypothesis and the calculations necessary to test H_0 depend on the test being carried out.

Whatever the test, the three steps for checking the hypothesis are the same. This is:

• Step 1 – Set up the null and alternative hypotheses and determine (usually from tables) the boundary or boundaries of the critical region. These boundaries are called the *critical values*. The critical values depend on whether the test is one or two tailed. The two-tailed test is used when you have no reason to suppose that the true mean could be either greater than or less than the value given by the null hypothesis. The one-tailed test is used when you are more interested in one side of the supposed mean than the other. Figures 8.1 and 8.2 make the distinction clearer.

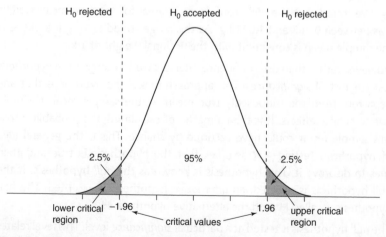

Figure 8.1 Two tailed test at the 5% significance level

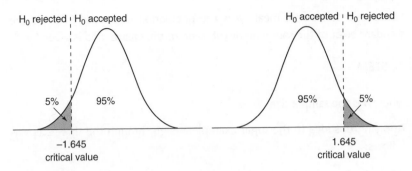

Figure 8.2 One tailed test at the 5% significance level

- Step 2 – Calculate the test statistic.
- Step 3 – Decide whether to accept or reject H_0

LARGE SAMPLE TEST FOR A POPULATION MEAN

The normal distribution can be used to solve problems involving means if the population is normal and the standard deviation of the population (σ) is known. If normality cannot be assumed then a large sample size will ensure that the sampling distribution of the means is approximately normal.

However, as in the calculation of confidence intervals (see Chapter 7) σ may be unknown and has to be estimated from the sample. In these cases the normal distribution can be used as an approximation, provided the sample size is large.

The formula for Z is also the same as that used in the derivation of the formula for confidence intervals. That is

$$Z = \frac{\overline{x} - \mu}{STEM}$$

where $\bar{x}$ is the sample mean, μ is the population mean and STEM is the standard error of the sampling distribution of the means, and is given by:

$$STEM = \frac{\sigma}{\sqrt{n}}$$

where n is the sample size

Applying this idea to the sugar example, we go through the three steps as follows:

• Step 1 – Set up H_0 and H_1 and decide on the critical values
  This is an example of a two-tailed test because we might be concerned with both over and underweight bags of sugar.

$H_0: \mu = 1\ kg \qquad H_1: \mu \neq 1\ kg$

From Figure 8.1 the critical values are ± 1.96

• Step 2 – Calculate the test statistic.
  In this problem, $n = 36$, $\mu = 1$, $\sigma = 0.056$ and $\bar{x} = 0.985$. Therefore

$$STEM = \frac{\sigma}{\sqrt{n}} = \frac{0.056}{\sqrt{36}}$$

$$= 0.09333$$

And

$$Z = \frac{\bar{x} - \mu}{STEM}$$

$$= \frac{0.985 - 1}{0.09333}$$

$$= -0.1607$$

This is the test statistic (the negative sign just means that the result is in the left hand part of the normal curve).

• Step 3 – Decide whether to accept or reject H_0

As Z (−0.1607) is greater than −1.96 (or 0.1607 is less than 1.96) it is in the acceptance region of the normal curve and we cannot reject H_0 and must conclude that there is no evidence that the sample mean is significantly different to 1 kg.

The next example illustrates the use of one tailed tests.

Example 8.1

The mean fuel consumption for a particular make of car is known to be 33 mpg with a standard deviation of 5.7 mpg. A modification to this car has been made that should reduce fuel consumption (it cannot be made worse). Thirty-five cars are fitted with this device and their fuel consumption is recorded over 12 months. At the end of this period the mean fuel consumption of the 35 cars is found to be 34.8 mpg. Is there any evidence, at the 5% level of significance, that the fuel consumption has been improved?

The null and alternative hypotheses for this problem are:

$H_0: \mu = 33$ mpg $H_1: \mu > 33$ mpg

and the critical value of Z at the 5% significance level is 1.645

$\sigma = 5.7$ mpg, $\bar{x} = 34.8$ and $n = 35$

Therefore, STEM $= \dfrac{5.7}{\sqrt{35}}$

$= 0.9635$

And the test statistic is: $Z = \dfrac{34.8 - 33}{0.9635}$

$= 1.868$

Since 1.868 is greater than the critical value of 1.645 (see Figure 8.3), you would reject the null hypothesis and accept the alternative hypothesis. That is, there is a significant difference between the mean fuel consumption before and after the modification has been fitted. You would conclude that the modification appears to have improved the fuel consumption of this particular make of car.

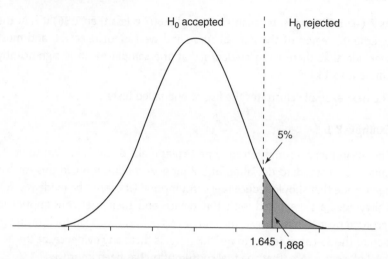

Figure 8.3 Hypothesis rejected (Example 8.1)

SMALL SAMPLE TEST FOR A POPULATION MEAN

As in the case of confidence intervals, it is necessary to assume that the population is normal and to use the t-distribution instead of the normal distribution. The formula for the t-statistic is the same as for the large sample case except that Z is replaced by t

$$t = \frac{\overline{x} - \mu}{STEM}$$

The formula for STEM is also the same, except that the standard deviation used is the estimate obtained from the sample.

The same considerations apply concerning the critical region, except that the critical value is obtained from the t-distribution on $n - 1$ degrees of freedom (Appendix 1). For example, the critical value on 7 degrees of freedom at the 5% significance level is ± 2.365 for a two-tailed test, and ± 1.895 for a one-tailed test.

The following example may help you understand the differences between the Z and t-tests.

Example 8.2

A tomato grower has developed a new variety of tomato. This variety is supposed to give good crops without the need for a greenhouse. One of the supposed attributes of this tomato is that the average yield per plant is at least 4 kg of fruit. A gardening magazine decides to test this claim and grows 8 plants in controlled conditions. The yield from each plant is carefully recorded and is as follows:

Plant	1	2	3	4	5	6	7	8
Yield	3.6	4.2	3.3	2.5	4.8	2.75	4.2	4.6

This is a one-tailed test, since the claim is that the yield should be at least 4 kg. The null and alternative hypotheses are therefore:

H_0: $\mu \geq 4$ kg H_1: $\mu < 4$ kg (The alternative hypothesis is less than 4 kg because the gardening magazine is attempting to disprove the claim.)

The critical value on 7 degrees of freedom at a significance level of 5% for a one-tailed test is −1.895. (This figure was obtained from the t-table in Appendix 1).

Estimates of the mean and standard deviation of the yield from this sample are:

$\bar{x} = 3.74$ $\sigma = 0.8466$

And STEM $= \dfrac{0.8466}{\sqrt{8}}$

$= 0.2993$

The test statistic (t) is therefore:

$\dfrac{3.74 - 4}{0.2993} = -0.869$

Since −0.869 is greater than −1.895 (see Figure 8.4), you cannot reject H_0 and the claim is justified.

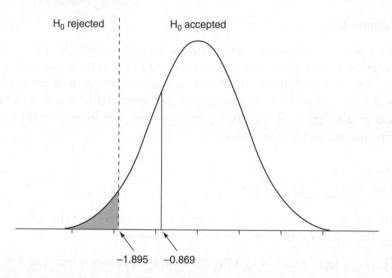

Figure 8.4 Hypothesis accepted (Example 8.2)

THE Z–TEST FOR A POPULATION PERCENTAGE

Testing a sample percentage against some expected or hypothesized value (π) is another important test. The test given here is based on the assumption that n is large and π is not too large or too small.

The standard error of the sampling distribution of a percentage (STEP) was given in Chapter 7 as:

$$\sqrt{\frac{P(100-P)}{n}}$$

where P is the sample percentage.

However, for hypothesis testing it is the population parameter, π, that must be used. With this substitution, the equation for STEP becomes:

$$\sqrt{\frac{\pi(100-\pi)}{n}}$$

The Z statistic is similar to that used for the test on a mean and is:

$$Z = \frac{P - \pi}{STEP}$$

Example 8.3

A trade union is considering strike action and intends to ballot its large membership on the issue. In order to gauge the likely result of the ballot, a survey was conducted among a random sample of members. Of the 60 people surveyed, 36 were in favour of a strike.

This gives a percentage of 60%, but is this figure significantly greater than 50% (for a simple majority)?

H_0: $\pi \leq 50\%$ H_1: $\pi > 50\%$

$$STEP = \sqrt{\frac{50(100 - 50)}{60}}$$

$$= 6.455$$

And the test statistic is:

$$Z = \frac{60 - 50}{6.455}$$

$$= 1.549$$

Since 1.549 is less than 1.645, H_0 cannot be rejected. That is, it appears that there may not be a majority for strike action.

HYPOTHESIS TESTS INVOLVING TWO POPULATION MEANS

The tests we have looked at so far are for a single sample. In many situations we may have collected two samples and we want to test to see if the two population means are the same. As in the single sample case we have different tests for large and small samples. We also have another factor to consider: are the samples independent of each other or not? Samples that are independent mean that the measurements of one sample are not influenced by the second sample. In some situations, once we have (randomly) chosen the members of the first sample the members of the second sample will not be independent. For example, you might want to compare the reading ability of children before and after following a reading programme. The reading scores of a group of children represent the first sample and the second sample is represented by the reading scores of the same children at the end of the reading programme. The second sample is therefore related to the first sample by the identity of the child. There are good reasons why you should use this paired approach, but it requires a test that doesn't demand independence.

Large sample tests for two independent population means

We normally wish to set up the null hypothesis that the difference in the means of the two populations will be zero; that is:

$H_0: \mu_1 - \mu_2 = 0$

The alternative hypothesis can again be either one or two tailed. That is:

$H_1: \mu_1 - \mu_2 \neq 0$ for a two-tailed test

$H_1: \mu_1 - \mu_2 > 0$ or $\mu_1 - \mu_2 < 0$ for a one-tailed test

For a large sample we can assume that the difference between the means of the two sampling distributions is normally distributed with a mean equal to the difference of the population means and a standard error of

$$\sigma_{(\bar{x}_1 - \bar{x}_2)} = \sqrt{\left(\frac{\sigma_1^2}{n_1} + \frac{\sigma_2^2}{n_2}\right)}$$

As in the single sample case, the population standard deviations are required, but provided that each sample size (n_1 and n_2) is at least 30 we can use the estimate given by the samples as an approximation.

The test statistic will be:

$$Z = \frac{(\bar{x}_1 - \bar{x}_2) - (\mu_1 - \mu_2)}{\sigma_{(\bar{x}_1 - \bar{x}_2)}}$$

Example 8.4

A high street store was interested in discovering whether store card customers spent more or less than other customers. A random sample of 50 store card customers were found to have spent £55.30 on average with a standard deviation of £18.45, while a random sample of 40 non-store card customers were found to have spent £52.75 on average with a standard deviation of £17.22

We could use this information to test if there was a difference in the amount spent by the different types of customers.

$H_0: \mu_1 - \mu_2 = 0$ $H_1: \mu_1 - \mu_2 \neq 0$

The standard error will be $\sqrt{\left(\dfrac{18.45^2}{50} + \dfrac{17.22^2}{40}\right)} = 3.7711$

And the test statistic will be $\dfrac{(55.30 - 52.75) - 0}{3.7711} = 0.676$

Since this is less than 1.96 we cannot reject H_0 and must conclude that there is no evidence to suggest that store card customers spend more or less than other customers.

Small sample tests for two independent population means

Just as in the single sample case we need to use the t-distribution instead of the normal. Both populations from which the samples have been taken should be approximately normally distributed with equal variances. The standard error for the small sample case is slightly different from that for large samples. It is:

$$\sigma_{(x_1 - x_2)} = \hat{\sigma} \sqrt{\left(\frac{1}{n_1} + \frac{1}{n_2} \right)}$$

where $\hat{\sigma}$ is the estimate of the *pooled* standard deviation of the populations

and is given by: $\hat{\sigma} = \sqrt{\dfrac{(n_1 - 1)s_1^2 + (n_2 - 1)s_2^2}{n_1 + n_2 - 2}}$

The test statistic is given by:

$$t = \frac{(\overline{x}_1 - \overline{x}_2) - (\mu_1 - \mu_2)}{\sigma_{(\overline{x}_1 - \overline{x}_2)}}$$

The critical value at a particular significance level and $(n_1 + n_2 - 2)$ degrees of freedom can be found from tables (see Appendix 1).

Example 8.5

A health magazine has decided to test the claim of the makers of a new slimming pill that has just come on the market. The company claims that the pill will allow people to lose weight if taken daily. The health magazine obtained a sample of 14 people who agreed to take the pill for a month. This group was split into two, a sample of 8 who would be given the slimming pill and a control group of 6 who would (unknown to them) be given a placebo (a fake slimming pill). The weight change at the end of the month is given in Table 8.1 where a minus indicates a loss of weight and a positive figure indicates a gain in weight.

It would of course be possible to apply the single sample test on the sample of 8 people to see if the mean weight change is different to zero. However, the use of a control group is quite common in medical research as it allows unknown factors such as people's 'belief' in a product to be taken into account.

Table 8.1 Weight change (in lbs)

Sample 1	Sample 2 (control group)
−2	−2
−6	5
3	−5
−10	8
0	4
2	0
−4	
−9	

If we assume that the health magazine is not biased in its opinion of the pill, this is a two-tailed test and the null and alternative hypotheses will be:

$$H_0: \mu_1 - \mu_2 = 0 \qquad H_1: \mu_1 - \mu_2 \neq 0$$

The mean and standard deviation for sample 1 are −3.25 and 4.862, respectively. The equivalent figures for the control group are 0.833 and 4.579, respectively. The pooled standard deviation is therefore:

$$\hat{\sigma} = \sqrt{\frac{(8-1)4.862^2 + (6-1)4.579^2}{8+6-2}}$$

$$= 4.746$$

And the standard error is

$$4.746\sqrt{\left(\frac{1}{8} + \frac{1}{6}\right)} = 2.563$$

The test statistic is $t = \dfrac{(-3.25 - 0.833) - 0}{2.563}$

$$= -1.593$$

The critical value on 12 degrees of freedom at 5% significance level is −2.179. As the test statistic is greater than this value we cannot reject H_0, so we conclude that there is no evidence that the slimming pill has any effect on weight change.

Paired samples

We have already mentioned that the two-sample t-test is only valid when the two samples are independent. In many cases this assumption is not valid as the data is paired; that is, each observation of one sample is paired with an observation in the other sample. This can occur if identical conditions apply to pairs of observations. The null hypothesis is that the difference of the population means, μ_d, is zero and the alternative hypothesis can be either one or two tailed, depending on whether we believe the difference could be positive, negative or not equal to zero. The test statistic for this test is:

$$t = \frac{\overline{x}_d - \mu_d}{\sigma_{\overline{d}}}$$

where $\overline{x}_d$ is the sample mean of the n differences and μ_d is the population mean difference if the null hypothesis is correct (usually zero). $\sigma_{\overline{d}}$ is the standard error of the differences and is given by:

$$\sigma_{\overline{d}} = \frac{s_d}{\sqrt{n}}$$

where s_d is the standard deviation of the differences.

Example 8.6

A publishing company has developed a new reading scheme that is supposed to improve the reading ability of children. In order to be able to justify its claim, 12 children were first given a standardized reading test before taking part in the programme. At the end of the programme they were tested again. The test scores before and after the programme can be found in Table 8.2.

Table 8.2 Test scores for Example 8.6

Child	Before	After	Difference
A	110	108	−2
B	121	122	1
C	95	98	3
D	80	90	10
E	130	132	2
F	100	105	5
G	105	105	0
H	85	90	5
I	95	96	1
J	100	98	−2
K	82	85	3
L	135	132	−3

The data are not independent because each member of the 'before' sample is related to a member of the 'after' sample by the attributes of the child. The advantage of this design is that it only looks at the differences between each child; it ignores the variation between children, which could be large. If the reading programme had had no effect you would expect the true average difference in test scores to be zero. The null hypothesis is therefore:

$$H_0: \mu_d = 0$$

The alternative hypothesis is one tailed because we are testing to see if the programme improves reading ability (it is unlikely to make it worse) so:

$$H_1: \mu_d > 0$$

The differences (after − before) can be found in Table 8.2, and the mean of the differences is 1.92 with a standard deviation of 3.655. The standard error of the differences is

$$\sigma_{\bar{d}} = \frac{3.655}{\sqrt{12}}$$

$$= 1.055$$

And the test statistic is $t = \dfrac{1.92 - 0}{1.055}$

$$= 1.820$$

The critical value of t at the 5% significance level and on 11 (12 – 1) degrees of freedom is 1.796. We can therefore reject H_0 at the 5% significance level and conclude that there is some evidence that the new reading programme does increase reading ability as represented by the testing method.

HYPOTHESIS TESTS INVOLVING TWO POPULATION PERCENTAGES

As well as conducting tests between two means it is possible to conduct tests between two percentages. Provided the sample sizes are large the difference between the two percentages ($\pi_1 - \pi_2$) will be normally distributed. The null hypothesis will be:

$H_0: \pi_1 - \pi_2 = 0$

And H_1 can be either one or two tailed.

The standard error of the differences between the two proportions is:

$$\sigma_{(P_1 - P_2)} = \sqrt{\hat{P}(100 - \hat{P})\left(\frac{1}{n_1} + \frac{1}{n_2}\right)}$$

where $\hat{P}$ is the estimate of the population proportion and is given by:

$$\hat{P} = \frac{n_1 P_1 + n_2 P_2}{n_1 + n_2}$$

P_1 and P_2 refer to the two sample proportions

The test statistic is:

$$Z = \frac{(P_1 - P_2) - (\pi_1 - \pi_2)}{\sigma_{(P_1 - P_2)}}$$

Example 8.7

A top hairdresser has just opened two hairdressing saloons in a large town and he is interested in whether there are any differences in the type of customers that use these two saloons. During one month a random sample of customers at both saloons were asked to complete a questionnaire. From the analysis of the questionnaire it was discovered that out of 200 customers at 'Top Cuts', 56 were under the age of 25. At 'Smart Cut's 54 out of 150 cuts were in this age bracket.

This is a two-tailed test and the null and alternative hypotheses are:

$$H_0: \pi_1 - \pi_2 = 0 \qquad\qquad H_1: \pi_1 - \pi_2 \neq 0$$

$$P_1 = \frac{56}{200} \times 100 \qquad\qquad P_2 = \frac{54}{150} \times 100$$

$$= 28\% \qquad\qquad = 36\%$$

$$\text{So } \hat{P} = \frac{200 \times 28 + 150 \times 36}{200 + 150}$$

$$= 31.4\%$$

The standard error of the differences is

$$\sigma_{(P_1 - P_2)} = \sqrt{31.4(100 - 31.4)\left(\frac{1}{200} + \frac{1}{150}\right)}$$

$$= 5.013$$

The test statistic is:

$$Z = \frac{(28 - 36) - 0}{5.013}$$

$$= -1.596$$

As this is greater than –1.96 we cannot reject H_0 and therefore conclude that there is no evidence to suggest that the percentage of customers in the under 25-age group is different in the two saloons.

THE χ^2 (CHI–SQUARE) HYPOTHESIS TEST

All the tests discussed so far in this chapter are called *parametric* tests in that they are testing a parameter (either the mean or proportion). However, there are also *non-parametric* tests and the text by *McClave* and *Sincich* (2006) contains many tests in this category. Perhaps the most useful non-parametric test is the χ^2 (pronounced 'chi-square') test and there are two forms of this test. The first form called the *goodness-of-fit* test tests to see if the data fits some distribution. The second form of the test is called the *test of association* and tests to see if there is any association between categories in a two-way table. For both forms of the tests you have to *count* the number of data items that are observed to be in a particular category. The test statistic is calculated using the following formula:

$$\sum \frac{(O-E)}{E}$$

where O represents the observed count and E represents the expected count. The formula simply says: 'Find the difference between the observed and expected frequency of one category, square this value to remove any negative signs and then divide by the expected frequency for that category. Repeat this for all categories and sum the individual answers'.

This test statistic follows the χ^2 distribution. The shape of this distribution depends on the degrees of freedom of the data. For example, for 4 degrees of freedom you would get the shape shown in Figure 8.5.

The area under the curve is again 1, but only one tail is used for the critical region – the upper tail. The area representing 5% has been indicated, and H_0 would be rejected if the test statistic was in this region.

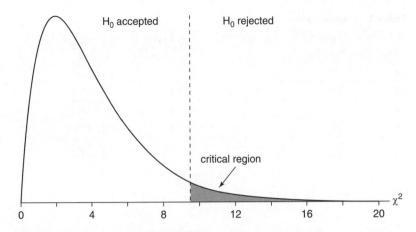

Figure 8.5 The chi-square distribution on 4 degrees of freedom

The critical value of χ^2 is found from the χ^2 table that you will find in Appendix 1. For example, the critical value on 4 degrees of freedom at the 5% (0.05) significance level is 9.488. The test statistic follows the χ^2 distribution providing the expected values are not too small. Anything below 5 is normally considered to be too small and if this occurs it is necessary to combine categories until this minimum number is achieved.

The 'goodness of fit' test

Suppose you threw a six-sided die 36 times. You would expect the faces numbered 1 to 6 to appear the same number of times; that is, 6. However, you might observe a rather different frequency such as the one below:

Face	1	2	3	4	5	6
Frequency	4	6	9	5	4	8

Is the observed frequency due to chance effects or does it indicate that the die is biased in any way? (In this example, face 3 occurs most.) The null hypothesis is that the die is fair and the alternate hypothesis is that it is biased; that is:

H_0: die is fair H_1: die is biased

Table 8.3 χ^2 calculation for die

O	E	O – E	(O – E)²	$\frac{(O – E)^2}{E}$
4	6	–2	4	0.667
6	6	0	0	0.000
9	6	3	9	1.500
5	6	–1	1	0.167
4	6	–2	4	0.667
8	6	2	4	0.667
			Sum	3.668

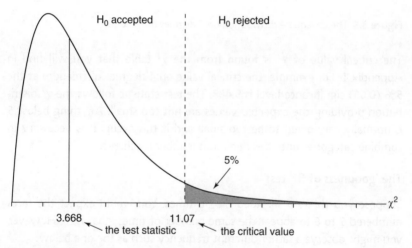

Figure 8.6 Hypothesis accepted (die was fair)

Since the sum of the frequencies is fixed, you are 'free' to choose 5 of them; therefore the degrees of freedom is 5. From the χ^2 table, the critical value on 5 degrees of freedom and at the 5% significance level is 11.070. If the test statistic is greater than this value, H_0 will be rejected.

To calculate the χ^2 statistic you need to subtract the observed values from 6, square the result and then divide by 6. This calculation is shown in Table 8.3.

The sum of these values is 3.668 and this is compared with the critical value of 11.070. H_0 cannot be rejected and you would have to assume that the die was fair. The diagram in Figure 8.6 demonstrates that the test statistic is not in the critical region.

The goodness-of-fit test can be used for any distribution providing you can obtain the expected values. So it is possible to check if a distribution fits a normal curve for example. The most important application of the χ^2 test is to test if there is any association between categories in a two-way table which we cover next.

Test of association

Example 8.8

The Personnel Manager of a company believes that monthly paid staff take more time off work through sickness than those staff who are paid weekly (and do not belong to the company sickness scheme). To test this theory, the sickness records for 561 randomly selected employees who have been in continuous employment for the past year were analysed. Table 8.4 was produced, which placed employees into 3 categories according to how many days they were off work through sickness during the past year. For example, 95 monthly paid employees were off sick for less than 5 days.

Table 8.4 is a usually called a *contingency* table. The null and alternative hypotheses are:

- H_0: There is no association between type of employee and number of days off sick.

- H_1: There is an association between type of employee and number of days off sick.

In order to calculate the χ^2 test statistic it is necessary to determine the expected values for each category. To do this you use the following formula:

$$\text{Expected value} = \frac{\text{Row total} \times \text{Column total}}{\text{Grand total}}$$

Table 8.4 Number of days off sick by type of employee

Type of employee	Number of days off sick			Total
	Less than 5 days	5 to 10 days	More than 10 days	
Monthly paid	95	47	18	160
Weekly paid	143	146	112	401
Total	238	193	130	561

Table 8.5 Calculation of the χ^2 test statistic

O	E	(O – E)	(O – E)²	$\frac{(O - E)^2}{E}$
95	67.9	27.1	734.41	10.816
47	55.0	−8.0	64.00	1.164
18	37.1	−19.1	364.81	9.833
143	170.1	−27.1	734.41	4.318
146	138.0	8.0	64.00	0.464
112	92.9	19.1	364.81	3.927
			Sum	30.522

These calculations are shown in Table 8.5.

The sum of the χ^2 values is 30.522, and this is the test statistic for this problem. The critical value depends on the degrees of freedom of this table. The formula for calculating the degrees of freedom is:

(number of columns − 1) × (number of rows − 1)

In Table 8.5, there are 3 columns (excluding the total column) and 2 rows, so the degrees of freedom are:

$(3-1) \times (2-1) = 2$

The critical value for 2 degrees of freedom at the 5% significance level is 5.991, and at the 0.1% significance level it is 13.815. Therefore, since the test statistic is greater than 13.815, H_0 can be rejected at the 0.1% significance level, and you could conclude that there does seem to be an association between staff category and the number of days off sick.

It is possible to be more specific about this association by looking at the individual χ^2 values and also the (O – E) column. The two largest χ^2 values are 10.816 and 9.883. These both relate to the monthly paid staff, which suggests that this group of employees has a higher frequency in the 'less than 5 days category' than expected but a lower frequency in the 'more than 10 days' category.

The χ^2 test for association is a very important and useful test in the area of statistics in particular, and decision-making in general. However, there are a couple of problems that you need to be aware of.

Two-by-two tables

The χ^2 distribution is a continuous distribution, whereas the sample data is discrete. Normally the sample size is sufficient to avoid making a continuity correction, but this will be needed for 2×2 tables. The correction required is to subtract 0.5 from the absolute value of the difference between the observed and expected values. For example, if the difference was –2.7, the corrected value would be –2.2 (not –3.2).

Tables of percentages

The χ^2 test is applied to tables of frequencies, not percentages. If you are given a table of percentages you will need to convert it to frequencies by multiplying each percentage by the total frequency. If you are not given the total frequency then it is not possible to use this test.

KEY POINTS

★ A hypothesis is formulated, and a test conducted on a sample of data in order to either accept or reject the hypothesis.

★ The test can either be two tailed or one tailed. We only use a one-tailed test when we are only interested in one side or tail of the mean or proportion.

★ Apart from the χ^2 test, the tests applied in this chapter are parametric tests – they test a parameter of a population.

★ The population parameters tested in this chapter include the mean and percentage. For tests of percentages, the sample size must be large.

★ For tests on the mean, a large sample allows the Z-distribution to be used; otherwise, it is necessary to use the t-distribution.

★ We can test a single mean or proportion or we can test two means or proportions. For a mean the test can either be two independent means or the samples can be paired.

★ The χ^2 test is used to test whether a frequency distribution follows some expected distribution, and can also be used to test whether there is an association between categories.

FURTHER READING

As with confidence intervals there are a large number of texts aimed at the business student. Chapter 9 of Oakshott (2012) uses a similar treatment to the one here. It also includes details of how to use Excel and SPSS in applying the tests. If you want to take the subject further McClave and Sincich (2006) is the 'gold standard' in this area. There is also an interesting article in Statistical Science by Tukey (1991).

REVISION QUESTIONS

1 A component produced for the electricity industry is supposed to have a mean outside diameter of 10 cm. The mean diameter of a sample of 36 components taken from today's output is 9.94 cm with a standard deviation of 0.018 cm. Does this suggest that the production process is not meeting the specifications?

2 A company has been accused of selling underweight products. This product is supposed to weigh 500 g; a sample of 6 was weighed and the results were:

495, 512, 480, 505, 490, 502

Is there any evidence that the mean weight is less than 500 g? (The weight of the product is known to be normally distributed.)

3 The Speedwell Building Society has claimed that there has been a significant increase in the percentage of its customers taking out fixed-rate mortgages. In the past, 30% of customers had this type of mortgage, but during the past week 60 out of 150 new mortgages have been at a fixed rate. Is the claim by the building society correct?

4 The number of accidents occurring at a large construction site during the past week has been as follows:

Mon	Tue	Wed	Thu	Fri
6	5	6	8	12

Is there any evidence that accidents are more likely on certain days of the week?

5 In Britain a survey was carried out of 171 radio listeners who were asked what radio station they listened to most during an average week. A summary of their replies is given below, together with their age range.

	Age range		
	Less than 20	20 to 30	Over 30
BBC	22	16	50
Local radio	6	11	16
Commercial	35	3	12

(a) Is there any evidence that there is an association between age and radio station?

(b) By considering the contribution to the value of your test, statistic from each cell and the relative sizes of the observed and expected frequencies in each cell indicate the main source of the association, if any exists.

9

CORRELATION AND REGRESSION

OBJECTIVES

- To be able to draw and interpret scatter diagrams
- To be able to calculate Spearman's rank correlation coefficient
- To be able to calculate Pearson's product moment correlation coefficient
- To understand and know how to use the least squares regression line
- To understand the limitations of these techniques

INTRODUCTION

The statistical analysis that you have covered so far has been concerned with the characteristics of a single variable. However, in some circumstances it might be of interest to look at two variables simultaneously – for instance, you might suspect that cost of production is dependent on the quantity produced, or that sales of a product are related to price. This chapter introduces two techniques: *correlation*, to measure the association between two variables, and *regression*, to obtain the relationship between the variables.

Fuel Inefficiency and Air Traffic Control (NATS)

In an ideal world an aircraft would take off reach cruising speed and then descend at the destination airport. Allowing for wind and other environmental factors this would give the minimum fuel burn. However in reality air traffic control has to amend flight paths and sometimes force aircraft to maintain a holding pattern until air space and/or runways are available. This means that aircraft use more fuel than necessary resulting in excess CO_2 omissions and increased cost.

The Operational Analysis (OA) team at NATS investigated the factors that affected excess fuel use so that a better understanding was obtained of the situation. The depended variable was the fuel inefficiency which was defined as the excess fuel used expressed as a fraction of the fuel used in the ideal case. Various independent variables were considered including:

- Track extension: As a result of changes to flight path
- Vertical inefficiency: when aircraft have to fly lower than the ideal altitude. This variable was further split into vertical inefficiency in climbing, cruising and in descent.

A correlation analysis was then conducted and it was found that both track extension and vertical inefficiency were both highly correlated with fuel inefficiency. There was also some weak to moderate correlation between the independent variables and to compensate for this some interaction affects were considered (see below)

Table 9.1 shows the 5 models that were considered by the OA team. Model A was the reference one as it represented the inefficiency normally considered in relation to fuel inefficiency. Each model was slightly more complex with model E containing all explanatory variables plus all interaction effects.

Table 9.1 Explanatory variables considered in regression models

Model	Explanatory variables considered					
	Relative track extension	Combined vertical inefficiency	Vertical inefficiency in climb	Vertical inefficiency in cruise	Vertical inefficiency in descent	Integration terms
A	X	–	–	–	–	–
B	X	X	–	–	–	X
C	X	–	X	X	X	–
D	X	–	X	X	X	X*
E	X	–	X	X	X	X

* only simple interaction affects considered

A regression analysis was carried out using two thirds of flights while the remaining one third of data was kept for validation purposes. The end result showed that while accuracy improved from model A to E there were serious issues concerned with model E and so this model was rejected. Model D was deemed the most appropriate and indicated that this model should be used for predicting fuel inefficiency.

Source: Hammond, S, et al, (2012), Air traffic control, business regulation and CO2 emissions, OR Insight, 25, 3, 127–149

SCATTER DIAGRAMS

A scatter diagram is simply a way of representing a set of bivariate data by a scatter of plots. One variable is plotted on the x-axis and the other on the y-axis. Normally the x variable (the independent variable) is the one that you believe influences the y variable (the dependent variable). That is y depends on x.

Examples of scatter diagrams are given in Figures 9.1 to 9.4. Figure 9.1 indicates a positive correlation because as the number of deliveries increases, so apparently does the delivery time. Figure 9.2 indicates a negative correlation because as the air temperature increases, the heating cost falls. Figure 9.3

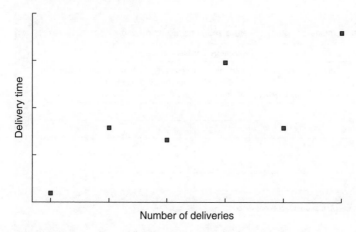

Figure 9.1 Positive correlation

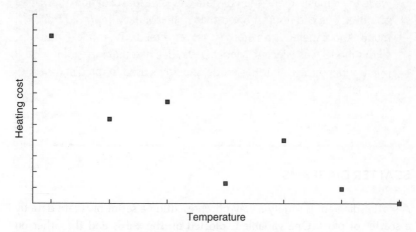

Figure 9.2 Negative correlation

suggests that no correlation exists between salary and age of employees. Figure 9.4 suggests that the quantity produced and the efficiency of a machine are correlated but not linearly.

When categorizing scatter diagrams you may find it easier to draw a closed loop around the points. This loop should be drawn so that it encloses all the points but at the same time makes the area within the loop as small as

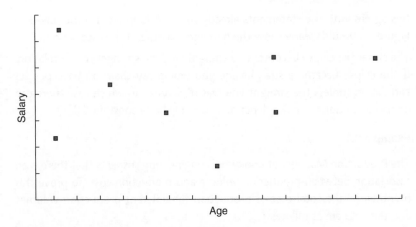

Figure 9.3 No correlation

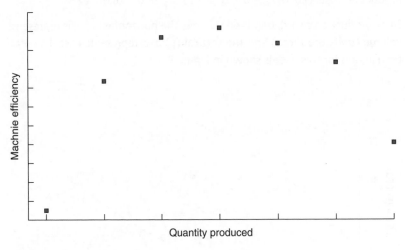

Figure 9.4 Nonlinear correlation

possible. If the loop looks like a circle, this suggests that there is little, if any, correlation, but if the loop looks more like an ellipse then this suggests that there is some correlation present. An ellipse pointing upwards would represent a positive correlation and one pointing downwards would represent a negative correlation. If you try this with Figures 9.1 to 9.3 you will see that this agrees with the statements already made. A loop around the points in Figure 9.4 would clearly show the non-linear nature of the association.

The closer the ellipse becomes to a straight line, the stronger the correlation. If the ellipse became a straight line you would say that you have perfect correlation (unless the straight line was horizontal, in which case there can be no correlation since the dependent variable has a constant value).

Example 9.1

The Production Manager at Lookwools Engineering suspects that there is an association between production volume and production cost. To prove this he obtained the total cost of production for different production volumes and the data are as follows:

Units produced (000s)	1	2	3	4	5	6
Production costs (£000s)	5.0	10.5	15.5	25.0	16.0	22.5

Since production cost depends on volume, the horizontal (x) axis represents volume (units produced) and the vertical (y) axis represents cost. The scatter diagram for this data is shown in Figure 9.5.

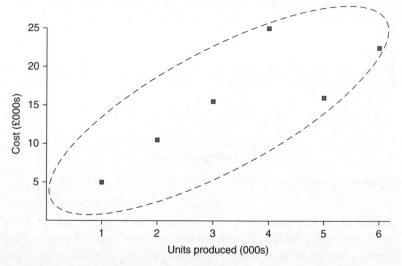

Figure 9.5 Scatter diagram for Lookwools Engineering (Example 9.1)

A closed loop has been drawn around the points and from this you should be able to make the following observations:

• There is a positive correlation between volume and cost.
• The loop is a fairly narrow ellipse shape suggesting that, for the range of data provided, the association is reasonably strong (but not perfect).
• If the point representing 4000 units was omitted the ellipse would be narrower.
• There is no evidence of non-linearity in the data.

Although these observations are valid, the sample size is rather small to make definite conclusions. In practice a larger sample size would be advisable (at least twelve pairs) and the cost of 4000 units would be checked. Sometimes these 'rogue' results suggest that other factors are influencing the dependent variable and further investigation is necessary.

CORRELATION

The technique of correlation measures the strength of the association between the variables. There are two widely used measures of correlation. These are *Spearman's rank correlation coefficient* and *Pearson's product moment correlation coefficient*. Both give a value between –1 and 1 so that –1 indicates a perfect negative correlation, 1 a perfect positive correlation and zero indicates no correlation. This is illustrated in Figure 9.6.

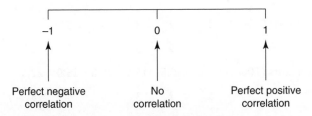

Figure 9.6 Range of values of the correlation coefficient

Spearman's rank correlation coefficient

This method involves ranking each value of x and y and using the following formula to calculate the coefficient R.

$$R = 1 - \frac{6\sum d^2}{n(n^2 - 1)}$$

where d is the difference in rank between pairs and n is the number of pairs. The value of R lies between 1 and –1.

The procedure to calculate this coefficient is as follows:

1. Rank both variables so that either the largest is ranked 1 or alternatively the smallest is ranked 1.

2. For each pair obtain the difference between the rankings.

3. Square these differences and sum.

4. Substitute the sum of these differences into the formula.

If during Step 1 you find you have equal rankings for the same variable, it is the mean of the rankings that is used. For example, if rank 3 occurs twice then both should be given a ranking of 3.5. The next ranking is 5

For example if you wanted to calculate Spearman's rank correlation coefficient for the data in Example 9.1 you would first rank the two variables as follows.

Units produced (000s)	1	2	3	4	5	6
Rank	1	2	3	4	5	6
Production costs (£000s)	5.0	10.5	15.5	25.0	16.0	22.5
Rank	1	2	3	6	4	5

You could then use a table (Table 9.2) to find R as follows:

Table 9.2 Calculation of Spearman's rank correlation coefficient (R)

No. of units	Cost	Difference (d)	d²
1	1	0	0
2	2	0	0
3	3	0	0
4	6	−2	4
5	4	1	1
6	5	1	1
		Sum	6

$$R = 1 - \frac{6 \times 6}{6 \times (6^2 - 1)}$$

$$= \frac{36}{6 \times 35}$$

$$= 0.829$$

This value is close to 1 which supports the assessment made from the scatter diagram that there is a fairly strong positive relationship between cost of production and production volume.

Data do not always consist of actual measurements. For example, in market research, data may consist of opinions on a particular product. This kind of data is called *ordinal* data. Ordinal data has the property that although it does not have actual numerical values, it can be ranked and therefore a correlation coefficient can be calculated.

Pearson's product moment correlation coefficient (r)

This measure of correlation tends to be the most popular, but it can only be used when the data is on the interval scale of measurement, that is, when the data consists of actual measurements. The formula for r is:

$$r = \frac{n \sum xy - \sum x \sum y}{\sqrt{[n \sum x^2 - (\sum x)^2][n \sum y^2 - (\sum y)^2]}}$$

Table 9.3   Calculation of the product moment correlation coefficient (r)

Units produced x	Production cost y	xy	x^2	y^2
1	5.0	5.0	1	25.00
2	10.5	21.0	4	110.25
3	15.5	46.5	9	240.25
4	25.0	100.0	16	625.00
5	16.0	80.0	25	256.00
6	22.5	135.0	36	506.25
$\sum x = 21$	$\sum y = 94.5$	$\sum xy = 387.5$	$\sum x^2 = 91$	$\sum y^2 = 1762.75$

We can demonstrate the use of this formula on the data in Example 9.1. Again the use of a table (Table 9.3) will help in setting out the calculations correctly. The summations can then be substituted into the formula for r.

$$r = \frac{6 \times 387.5 - 21 \times 94.5}{\sqrt{[6 \times 91 - (21)^2][6 \times 1762.75 - (94.5)^2]}}$$

$$= \frac{340.5}{\sqrt{(105 \times 1646.25)}}$$

$$= \frac{340.5}{415.7599}$$

$$= 0.8190$$

This calculation agrees with Spearman's calculation (0.829) in that there is a strong positive correlation between production volume and cost.

Pearson's product moment correlation coefficient is a more accurate measure of the correlation between two numeric variables. However, it cannot be applied to non-numeric data.

LINEAR REGRESSION

The technique of linear regression attempts to define the relationship between the dependent and independent variables by the means of a linear equation. This is the simplest form of equation between two variables and, fortunately, many situations can at least be approximated by this type of relationship.

The scatter diagram for the production cost data of Example 9.1 has been reproduced in Figure 9.7. You will see that a line has been drawn through the data and this line represents the linear relationship between the two variables. However, since the relationship is not perfect it is possible to draw several different lines 'by eye' through the diagram, each of which would look reasonable. However, each line would represent a slightly different relationship as the gradient and/or intercept on the *y*-axis would be different. To decide how good a particular line is, you could find the difference between each point and the line. These differences are often referred to as the 'errors' between the actual value and that predicted by the line.

These errors have been represented by vertical lines on the diagram. Note that the errors below the line are negative and those above the line are positive. If you add these errors you will find that the total error is zero. Does this prove that the line is a good one? Unfortunately not, because the zero

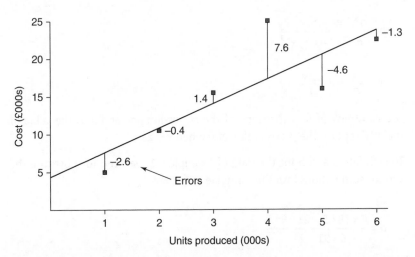

Figure 9.7 Line of best fit drawn though Lookwools Engineering data (Example 9.1)

value is only obtained by adding positive and negative values. Many more lines could be found that also would give a total error of zero. The errors could be added, ignoring the sign, but it can be shown that the best line or the 'line of best fit' is obtained when the sum of the squares of the errors is minimized. Squaring the errors not only removes the minus sign, but also gives more emphasis to the large errors.

Linear regression involves finding that line that minimizes the sum of squares of the errors. The theory behind the method of least squares is beyond the scope of this book, but the application of the theory is straightforward. The most important part is to ensure that the y variable is the dependent variable – so, for example, the production cost depends on the number of units produced.

The linear regression model is given in the form:

$$y = a + bx$$

where a and b are constants. The values of a and b that minimize the squared errors are given by the equations:

$$b = \frac{n\sum xy - \sum x \sum y}{n\sum x^2 - (\sum x)^2}$$

$$a = \frac{\sum y}{n} - b\frac{\sum x}{n}$$

You can think of b as the slope of the regression line and a as the value of the intercept on the y-axis (value of y when x is zero).

To calculate a and b for the data of Example 9.1 we need to substitute the various summations into the formulae as follows:

$$b = \frac{6 \times 387.5 - 21 \times 94.5}{6 \times 91 - 21^2}$$

$$= 3.2429$$

and

$$a = \frac{94.5}{6} - \frac{(3.2429 \times 21)}{6}$$

$$= 4.3999$$

The regression equation for this data is therefore:

$$y = 4.4 + 3.24x$$

This suggests that for every 1 unit (1000) rise in production volume, the production cost would rise by, on average 3.24 units (£3 240) and that when nothing is produced ($x = 0$), the production cost would still be £4 400. This probably can be explained by factory overhead costs that are incurred even when there is no production.

To use this equation you simply substitute the relevant production volume for x. So if production volume was 2500 units the cost would be:

$$y = 4.4 + 3.24 \times 2.5$$

$$= 12.5; \text{ that is } £12,500$$

When using a regression equation it is important that you don't try using the equation outside the range of data used to fit the equation. So trying to find the cost of a production volume of 20,000 units would not be appropriate as it is well outside the range (maximum was 6,000 units).

COEFFICIENT OF DETERMINATION

Before a regression equation can be used effectively as a predictor for the dependent variable, it is necessary to decide how well it fits the data. One statistic that gives this information is the *coefficient of determination*. This measures the proportion of the variation in the dependent variable explained by the variation in the independent variable. It is given by r^2, which is the square of the product moment correlation coefficient. So for the production cost data the value of $r^2 = (0.8190)^2$ which is 0.67. So this means that 67% of the variation of in production cost is explained by the production volume. Alternatively 33% of the variation is unexplained.

KEY POINTS

★ A dependent variable is a variable that depends on one or more other (independent) variables.

★ The correlation between the dependent and an independent variable can be either positive or negative, depending on whether the dependent variable increases or decreases with an increase in the independent variable.

★ Spearman's correlation coefficient can be calculated on any bivariate data but it is normally used for ordinal data.

★ Pearson's product moment correlation coefficient can only be used on interval scale data.

★ Given a value of the independent variable, a linear regression model allows the value of the dependent variable to be calculated.

★ The method of least squares is used to calculate the parameters in a linear regression model.

★ The coefficient of determination determines what proportion of the variability in the dependent variable is explained by the independent variable.

FURTHER READING

There are a large number of texts on this topic at varying levels. Many texts such as Morris (2008) and, Curwin and Slater (2008) are aimed at the business student. Chapter 10 of Oakshott (2012) gives a similar coverage to this one and also includes details of how to use Excel and SPSS when analysing bivariate data. A useful text for the student with good maths skills is the one by Anderson, Sweeney and Williams (2007) but it goes way beyond what most business students need.

REVISION QUESTIONS

1 Suppose the correlation coefficient for age and earnings is 0.3. With the help of a sketch explain what this means. Define the age range to which this correlation might apply

2 Consider the following pairs of variables and make an assessment of the likely correlation between them. Mark each pair to show whether you expect the correlation to be positive or negative (strong or weak), or close to zero:
   (a) Attendance totals and position in football league table
   (b) The age of a relatively new make of car and its value
   (c) The age of a vintage make of car and its value
   (d) Length of education and annual earnings
   (e) Level of unemployment and hire purchase sales over a period of 10 years2

3 Calculate Spearman's correlation coefficient for the following data.

x	1	2	3	4	5	6	7
y	9	6	7	9	5	2	1

4 The data in the table below relate to the weight and height of a group of students.
   (a) Draw a scatter diagram of weight against height for the whole data. Alongside each point write either 'm' or 'f' as appropriate.

Height (in)	Weight (lb)	Sex
68	148	male
69	126	female
66	145	male
70	158	male
66	140	female
68	126	female
64	120	female
66	119	female
70	182	male
62	127	female
68	165	male
63	133	male
65	124	female
73	203	male

(b) Describe your scatter diagram. Try drawing an ellipse around
   (i) all the points
   (ii) the points relating to the male students
   (iii) the points relating to the female students.

Is there any indication that the correlation is stronger for either group?

(c) Calculate Pearson's product moment correlation coefficient for the three sets of points identified in (b) above. Comment on the values obtained.

5 A company is investigating the relationship between sales and advertising revenue. Data has been collected on these two variables and is shown below (all figures are in £000s):

	Jan	Feb	Mar	Apr	May	Jun	Jul	Aug	Sep	Oct	Nov	Dec
Sales	60	60	58	45	41	33	31	25	24	23	23	23
Adv.	6.0	6.0	6.0	5.8	4.5	4.1	3.3	3.1	2.5	2.4	2.3	2.3

(a) Plot a scatter diagram of the data given in the table above. Comment on the strength of the association between the two variables.

(b) Obtain the least squares regression line and comment on how well it fits the data.

(c) What would the expected sales be, given an advertising expenditure of £5000?

10

INVESTMENT APPRAISAL

OBJECTIVES

- To understand the reasons for investment appraisal
- To know how to select projects on the basis of their payback periods
- To be able to calculate the accounting rate of return
- To be able to discount a future sum of money
- To know how to select projects on the basis of their net present value
- To be able to calculate the internal rate of return for a project
- To understand the limitations of each method

INTRODUCTION

Companies are frequently faced with the need to decide between a number of investment opportunities. As capital is usually limited, a company will want to choose the 'best' project or projects. But what do we mean by 'best', and how can we differentiate between different projects that may look equally attractive?

The projects considered in this chapter are those that require an initial capital outlay and then generate income over several years. The life of a project is of paramount importance as a sum of money that will be generated in the future will not be so attractive as money that is available in the present. This chapter looks at several methods that can be used to determine the worth of an investment.

Syngenta Grangemouth Expansion

Syngenta is a world leading agriculture business and its mission is "bringing plant potential to life". It uses the latest science and technology to develop products that will improve plant productivity. One of its best selling brands is Amistar, which is one of the most popular fungicide products in the world. Because of the popularity of this product the company has in the past not been able to meet the demand and so consideration was given to increase manufacturing capacity by building a new plant at its Grangemouth site in Scotland. Because the plant would cost £150m the company needed to be sure that this would be a profitable investment. They therefore went through an *investment appraisal* process. This involved analysing the inflows and outflows of the project to ensure that the investment would produce value for shareholders and for the long term future of the company. Table 10.1 gives the type of data that Syngenta would have used for their analysis.

Table 10.1 Estimated cash flows for Syngenta Grangemouth expansion project (cash flows in £m)

	Year 0	Year 1	Year 2	Year 3	Year 4	Year 5	Year 6	Year 7	Year 8	Year 9
Total inflow		200	400	400	400	400	400	400	400	400
Cash outflow										
Investment	150									
Manufacturing costs		80	160	160	160	160	160	160	160	160
Sales and marketing		15	30	30	30	30	30	30	30	30
Other costs		25	25							
Total outflow	150	120	215	190	190	190	190	190	190	190
Net cash flow	(150)	80	185	210	210	210	210	210	210	210

Source: Copyright Business Case Studies LLP. Reproduced by permission of the publisher. www.businesscasestudies.co.uk (illustrative data only)

The investment appraisal methods that Syngenta used included:

1. Payback period
2. Average rate of return
3. Net present value (NPV)

The payback method is simply the time it takes to pay back the initial investment. At the end of year 2 the project has paid back £265m (80 + 185) which exceeds the £150m initial outlay. So the payback period is less than 2 years.

The average rate of return is the average profit expressed as a percentage of the initial outlay. For this project the total outflows was £1,815m and the total inflows was £3,400m giving a net cash inflow of £1,585m. If this figure is divided by 9 (the project's projected life) the average of £176.1m is obtained. As a percentage of £150m this is 117.4% which is extremely good and no other investment (such as bank deposits) could achieve anywhere near this rate.

For both these methods it is assumed that the future value of money is the same as the value today. The final method uses discounted cash flow (DCF) to represent the future value of money. For this method it was necessary to decide on the *discount* rate. The discount rate is the minimum return expected on the capital employed. Using a rate of 20% the discounted cash flows over the 9 years is shown in Table 10.2

Table 10.2 Discounted cash flows for Syngenta Grangemouth expansion project

	Year 0	Year 1	Year 2	Year 3	Year 4	Year 5	Year 6	Year 7	Year 8	Year 9
Net cash flow £m	(150)	80	185	210	210	210	210	210	210	210
DCF £m	(150)	66.4	127.7	121.8	100.8	84.0	71.4	58.8	48.3	39.9

Source: Copyright Business Case Studies LLP. Reproduced by permission of the publisher. www.businesscasestudies.co.uk (illustrative data only)

Adding up these DCF (remembering that the 150 is negative) we get a figure of £569.1m. As this figure is positive this project is better than using the £150m for an alternative project yielding a return of only 20%.

On the basis of this analysis the Grangemouth expansion project was approved and came on stream in 2010.

All these investment appraisal methods will be looked at in detail in the rest of this chapter.

Source: The Times 100 Business Case Studies

MEASURES OF INVESTMENT WORTH

You may think that it should be easy to judge the worth of an investment. Surely the larger the profit that will be generated, the better? Unfortunately it is not so simple as this because two projects could generate the same total profit but be quite different in the pattern of cash flows. Example 10.1 illustrates a typical case.

Example 10.1

BAS Holdings specializes in the development of out-of-town shopping centres. It is currently investigating three possible projects and these are located at Andover (A), Bristol (B) and Carlisle (C). The sites at Andover and Bristol require an investment of £4m each while the site at Carlisle requires an investment of £5m. Income from rents is guaranteed for up to 5 years, after which time BAS Holdings will transfer ownership to the local council. The net cash flows are given in Table 10.3, where year 0 refers to 'now'.

In Example 10.1 the company has to decide which, if any, of the projects to accept. Even if all projects are profitable the company may not have the resources to proceed with them all. Perhaps it should compare each project in terms of the profit made at the end of the 5 years (4 years in the case of Bristol).

Table 10.3 Cash flows for Example 10.1

Year	Andover (£m)	Bristol (£m)	Carlisle (£m)
0	−4.0	−4.0	−5.0
1	1.0	1.5	0.0
2	1.0	2.5	0.5
3	1.0	0.5	1.5
4	1.0	0.5	2.0
5	1.0	0.0	3.0

Table 10.4 Calculation of total profits

Year	Andover (£m)	Bristol (£m)	Carlisle (£m)
0	−4.0	−4.0	−5.0
1	1.0	1.5	0.0
2	1.0	2.5	0.5
3	1.0	0.5	1.5
4	1.0	0.5	2.0
5	1.0	0.0	3.0
Profit	1.0	1.0	2.0

The profit is simply the sum of the cash flows over the life of each project and they are shown in Table 10.4

On the basis of total profit the Carlisle project is best, but this project also has the largest initial investment and income is not generated until year 2. Andover and Bristol give the same profit, but notice how differently the earnings are generated. Bristol gives larger cash flows at the start, but no earnings are received in year 5, whereas Andover gives a constant flow of earnings for the full 5 years.

You should now appreciate that deciding on the best project is not a simple matter. There are several methods that can be used to compare projects and these fall into two categories. The first category is often termed 'traditional' and involves accounting procedures that do not take into account the time value of money. The second method involves procedures that discount future sums of money.

TRADITIONAL METHODS FOR COMPARING PROJECTS

There are two main methods in this category. These are the *payback* method and the *accounting rate of return* (ARR). The payback method simply tells you how long it takes for the original investment to be repaid. So on this basis project A takes 4 years, B takes 2 years and C takes 4 years. This indicates that the Bristol project is to be preferred since it takes less time for the original investment to be repaid.

The payback method is an easily understood method and favours projects that generate large cash flows early. This is an advantage since early cash flows will help a company's liquidity and also minimize risks of unforeseen problems in the future. However, this method ignores cash flows that are generated after the payback period. For example, with project C large cash flows are generated in years 4 and 5 and this is not taken into account with the payback method.

The accounting rate of return (sometimes called the return on capital employed) is the ratio of average annual income to the initial outlay and can be expressed as follows:

$$ARR = \frac{\text{Average income (per year)}}{\text{Initial outlay}} \times 100\%$$

For project A the average income is £5m/5 = £1m and the initial outlay is £4m so the ARR = $\frac{1}{4} \times 100$

$$= 25\%$$

For project B the average income will again be £1m. Since the capital employed is £4m, the ARR is again 25%.

For project C the average income is: £1.4 m, the initial outlay is £5 m so the ARR in this case is 28%

On the basis of the ARR, Project C is the better project.

The ARR is easy to calculate but it has many disadvantages, such as not allowing for timing of the cash flows. For example, project A and project B are ranked equal even though project B generates larger cash flows in the first two years.

DISCOUNTED CASH FLOW TECHNIQUES

The disadvantages of the payback and the ARR methods are that they do not take into account the time value of money; that is, money in the future is not worth as much as money now. So we need some method of *discounting* future sums of money. In order to understand the idea of discounting, it is first necessary to revise the idea of simple and compound interest. *Simple interest* is the expression used when interest on a sum of money is calculated on the principal only. This situation occurs when the interest is withdrawn as it is earned. So if you invested £10,000 in an investment account paying 2% p.a the interest each year is simply 2% of £10,000 which is £200.

Compound interest is when the interest is reinvested so the principal increases. So at the end of the 1st year the principal has increased to £10,200 and the interest at the end of the 2nd year would be 2% of £10,200 which is £204. Rather than having to do this calculation repeatedly you can use the following compound interest formula:

$$P_n = P_0 \left(1 + \frac{r}{100}\right)^n$$

Where P_0 = initial principal

P_n = the principal after n years

r is the interest rate

So after 5 years the initial principal of £10,000 at 2% interest rate will be worth

$$p_5 = 10000 \times \left(1 + \frac{2}{100}\right)^5$$

$$= £11,040.81$$

This calculation can also be carried out in reverse; that is, if you know a future sum of money you can find out how much it will be worth now given a fixed interest rate. To do this the compound interest formula is changed to make P_0 the subject. That is:

$$P_0 = P_n \times \frac{1}{\left(1+\dfrac{r}{100}\right)^n}$$

The expression $\dfrac{1}{\left(1+\dfrac{r}{100}\right)^n}$ is called the *discount factor*. So if $r = 2\%$ and $n = 4$ years the discount factor would be:

$$\frac{1}{(1.02)^4} = 0.9238$$

So the discounted value of £30,000 would be $30000 \times 0.9238 = £27,714$.

The figure £27,714 is called the *present value* of £30,000 and the 2% is called the *discount rate*.

Net present value

In Example 10.1 income was received each year for 5 years. To find the present value of this income stream we could find the present value of each yearly amount and add them up to get the present value of the total for 5 years. The discount rate is the rate the company could get from alternatives investments. Let us assume this is a healthy 8%. This means that the discount factor for year 1 would be $\dfrac{1}{1.08} = 0.9259$. So using project B as an example the income for year 1 is £1.5 m and the present value of £1.5 m is $1.5 \times 0.9259 = £1.3889$ m. If this is repeated for each year we get Table 10.5.

Table 10.5 Calculation of present value for project B

Year	Discount factor	Income (£m)	Present value (£m)
1	0.9259	1.5	1.3889
2	0.8573	2.5	2.1433
3	0.7938	0.5	0.3969
4	0.7350	0.5	0.3675
5	0.6806	0.0	0.0
Total			4.2966

Table 10.6 Calculation of present value for all three projects

Year	Discount factor	Andover Cash flow (£m)	Andover Present value (£m)	Bristol Cash flow (£m)	Bristol Present value (£m)	Carlisle Cash flow (£m)	Carlisle Present value (£m)
0		−4.0		−4.0		−5.0	
1	0.9259	1.0	0.9259	1.5	1.3889	0.0	0.0
2	0.8573	1.0	0.8573	2.5	2.1433	0.5	0.4287
3	0.7938	1.0	0.7938	0.5	0.3969	1.5	1.1907
4	0.7350	1.0	0.7350	0.5	0.3675	2.0	1.4700
5	0.6806	1.0	0.6806	0.0	0.0	3.0	2.0418
Total			3.9926		4.2966		5.1312
NPV			−0.0740		0.2966		0.1312

The last column of Table 10.5 gives the total present value. As project B required a £4m outlay the *net present value* is 4.2966 − 4 = 0.2966 or £296,000.

The net present value (or NPV) represents how good an investment it is. If positive it means that this project is better than an alternative investment yielding 8%, if negative it is worse and if zero there is no difference. So on this basis project B is a viable project. However we now need to compare it with the NPV of the other two projects. The details are shown in Table 10.6

On the basis of the NPV, project A would result in a loss and is therefore not a profitable investment, while project B is the most profitable investment.

Internal rate of return

The NPV method is a very useful method as it takes into account the timing of a series of cash flows. However, the decision is dependent on the discount rate used – a larger rate will reduce the NPV and could change the decision from accept to reject. An alternative approach is to calculate the discount rate that will give the NPV of zero. This is called the *Internal Rate of Return* or IRR. If the IRR for a project is greater than or equal to the cost of capital for a company, the project would be acceptable; if not, the project should be rejected. In the case of BAS Holdings, the cost of capital is 8% and any project with an IRR of at least this figure will be acceptable. Calculation of the IRR is not straightforward but an approximate value can be obtained using either a graphical approach or a linear interpolation. For both methods you need to calculate the NPV for two different discount rates. For the greatest accuracy the NPVs should be small, and preferably one should be positive and one negative. For the graphical method these points are plotted on a graph of NPV against discount rate and a line drawn between them. The point where the line crosses the horizontal axis (which represents zero NPV) can then be read from the graph. To use the interpolation method the following formula can be used:

$$IRR = \frac{N_1 r_2 - N_2 r_1}{N_1 - N_2}$$

Where an NPV of N_1 was obtained using a discount rate of r_1 and an NPV of N_2 was obtained using a discount rate of r_2

We shall demonstrate this interpolation method using project B. As this gave a positive NPV the IRR must be greater than 8%. Therefore we shall try 11%. You should find that this gives an NPV of £0.0754 which is positive and so the IRR must be greater than 11%. If we now try 13% we find that the NPV is −£0.0614 so the IRR must be between 11% and 13%. Using the interpolation formula we get

$N_1 = 0.0754$, $r_1 = 11\%$ and $N_2 = -0.0614$, $r_2 = 13\%$

So IRR = $\dfrac{0.0754 \times 13 - (-0.0614) \times 11}{0.0754 - (-0.0614)}$

= 12.1%

Table 10.7 Summary of the different methods of investment appraisal

Method	Project			Decision
	A	B	C	
Payback	4 years	2 years	4 years	B
ARR	25%	25%	28%	C
NPV	−£0.0074m	£0.2966m	£0.1312m	B
IRR	7.93%	12.1%	8.66%	B

If you try this method for Projects A and C you should get an IRR of 7.93% and 8.66% respectively.

The results of the IRR calculations agree with the NPV method; that is, project A is not profitable, while project B appears to be more profitable than project C. The advantage of the IRR method is that it allows you to have a benchmark against which projects can be measured, and a rate of return is something that management understand. The disadvantages are that it is more difficult to calculate and does not take into account the absolute value of the cash flows. So, on the basis of IRR, a project giving an NPV of £100 might look better than a project with an NPV of £1m. Table 10.7 summarizes the four different methods of investment appraisal for Example 10.1.

KEY POINTS

★ Traditional accounting procedures do not take time into account. Examples of such methods are the payback method and the accounting rate of return.

★ Compound interest is normally applied to an investment as this means that the interest also gains interest.

★ The compound interest formula can be re-arranged so that you can work out the amount of money you need to invest now that will give you a desired sum of money in *n* years time.

★ Put another way this means that you can calculate what a sum of money in *n* year's time is worth at today's prices. This is called the discounted cash flow technique and allows investments that mature at different times to be compared more easily.

★ When we subtract the initial outlay we get the net present value.

★ A net present value greater than zero means that a project is worthwhile

★ The internal rate of return gives the discount rate that makes the net present value zero.

FURTHER READING

Investment appraisal is a huge subject and is treated differently depending on the background of the authors. So an accountant would look at the subject differently from an economist and a tax expert would also have a different approach. Chapter 12 of Oakshott (2012) gives a similar coverage to this text. For a general text that covers the material in this chapter and extends it further, but in a non-mathematical manner, the one by Lumby and Jones (1999) is a good choice.

REVISION QUESTIONS

1 The following cash flows occur with 3 different investment opportunities. Use the payback method and the accounting rate of return to decide which is the best investment opportunity.

Year	Investment A	Investment B	Investment C
0	−20	−15	−5
1	12	0	3
2	10	10	3
3	5	5	3
4	3	5	3
5	0	5	3

2 What is the present value of £50 000 that is payable in 5 years' time if interest rates are expected to be constant at 6% during this period?

3 Using the cash flows given in Question 1 and the NPV method of investment appraisal, decide which (if any) of the three investment opportunities should be undertaken. Assume a discount rate of 6%.

4 A machine is purchased for £3750 and generates a revenue of £1310 per year for 5 years. After this time, it ceases to be productive and has no scrap value.

    (a) Assuming a discount rate of 11.2 %, calculate its net present value.

    (b) Find a discount rate at which the net present value becomes negative, and use it to estimate the internal rate of return.

5 A firm is considering the purchase of one of two machines. The first (machine A), costing £4000, is expected to bring in revenues of £2000, £2500 and £1500 respectively in the 3 years for which it will be operative; while the second (machine B), which costs £3900, will produce revenues of £1500, £2500 and £2000, and has the same lifetime. Neither machine will have any appreciable scrap value at the end of its life. Assuming a discount rate of 8%, compare and contrast different methods for evaluating which machine should be purchased. (Hint to calculating IRRs: a discount rate of 25% gave NPVs of −£32 and −£76 for machines A and B respectively.)

11

TIME SERIES ANALYSIS

OBJECTIVES

- To be able to apply the technique of moving averages to isolate the trend in a time series
- To understand the circumstances in which the additive and multiplicative models should be used
- To be able to calculate the seasonal component for both the additive and multiplicative models
- To know how to apply the technique of exponential smoothing in appropriate circumstances
- To be able to make forecasts, and to understand the limitations of these forecasts

INTRODUCTION

Many variables have values that change with time, such as the weekly sales of ice cream, visits abroad by UK residents, or the daily production rates for a factory. The changing value of such variables over a period of time is called a *time series*. The analysis of time series data is very important both for industry and for government, and a large number of people are employed to do this analysis. This chapter will look at the main features of a time series, and demonstrate some popular techniques.

Predicting Ambulance Demand in Wales

The Welsh Ambulance Service Trust (WAST) uses a range of quantitative techniques to efficiently employ ambulances so as quality targets are met. However these techniques are of little use if forecasts of patient demand are inaccurate. A group from Cardiff University researched different methods to find the one that would give the best forecasts.

While all medical services have limited resources the demand for these services are increasing. This is particularly the case in Wales for their Emergency Medical Service (EMS) which is facing a higher increase for its services than for the UK as a whole. Figure 11.1 shows the daily demand over a 5 year period. The peaks represent January 1st of each year. A trend line has been drawn in which shows that there is an increasing upward trend over these 5 years.

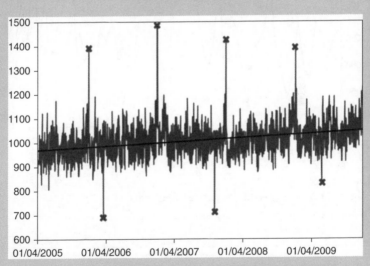

Figure 11.1 WAST daily demand (1 April 2005–31 December 2009)

Source: JL Vile et al (2012) 'Predicting ambulance demand using singular spectrum analysis', *Journal of the Operational Research Society* 63, 1556–1565.

A number of different models were tried including Holt Winters (a form of exponential smoothing) but the one that was chosen was called Singular Spectrum Analysis (SSA). This is quite a complex model and is not covered in this chapter but it is used extensively in climatic time series. Figure 11.2 compares the forecasts for each model and this chart shows that SSA follows the true demand quite well.

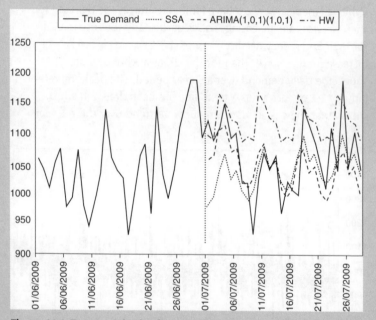

Figure 11.2 Twenty-eight day forecasts beginning on 1 July 2009

Source: JL Vile et al. (2012). Predicting ambulance demand using singular spectrum analysis. *Journal of the Operational Research Society* 63, 1556–1565

TIME SERIES MODELS

There are a large number of time series models including the ones mentioned in the case study above. We will however look at two of the simplest ones; these are the *decomposition* model and *exponential forecasting*. The further reading section will provide readers with books that take the subject to a more comprehensive level.

The decomposition model

This model assumes that a time series is made up of several components. These components are:

- Trend
- Seasonality
- Cyclic behaviour
- Randomness

The trend represents the long-run behaviour of the data and can be increasing, decreasing or constant. Seasonality relates to periodic fluctuations that repeat themselves at fixed intervals of time. Cyclic behaviour represents the ups and downs of the economy or of a specific industry. It is a long-term fluctuation and for practical purposes is usually ignored. Randomness is always present in a time series and represents variation that cannot be explained. Some time series (for example, share prices) have a very high random component and the forecasts of these series will be subject to a high degree of error.

Example 11.1

Table 11.1 consists of the sales of sun cream by Mace Skin Care plc.

Figure 11.3 is a plot of the data in Table 11.1. From this chart you should be able to see a strong seasonal component since the patterns repeat themselves at regular intervals with a peak in quarter 3 and a trough in quarter 1. You should also notice that the sales of sun cream appear to have increased rapidly during the 3-year period.

Table 11.1   Sales of sun cream

Year	Quarter	Sales (£000s)
2011	1	6.00
	2	9.00
	3	12.00
	4	8.00
2012	1	8.00
	2	13.50
	3	17.00
	4	13.00
2013	1	12.00
	2	20.25
	3	30.00
	4	19.50
2014	1	18.00

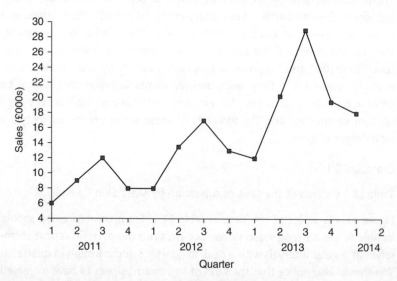

Figure 11.3 Sales of sun cream by Mace Skin Care plc

Isolating the trend

To isolate the trend you need to remove the seasonal fluctuations. This is done by a technique called *moving averages*. To use this technique you need to identify the period when the series repeats itself and to have a set number of data values within this repeating series. So in the sun cream example the data is in quarters and repeats itself every 4 quarters. You calculate the average for the first 4 quarters and then move along by one quarter to repeat the calculation. So the first average would be $(6 + 9 + 12 + 8)/4 = 8.75$; the second average would be $(9 + 12 + 8 + 8)/4 = 9.25$ and so on. Before these moving averages can be used they need to be *centred* because they don't currently correspond to an actual quarter (the 8.75 value corresponds to the middle of the year). If the average of 8.75 and 9.25 is used ($= 9.00$) this value can be plotted alongside quarter 3. Table 11.2 and Figure 11.4 make this clear. (Note: the moving averages in Table 11.2 have been added alongside a quarter for ease).

Table 11.2 Moving averages for the sun cream example

Year	Quarter	Sales £000s)	Moving average	Centered moving average
2011	1	6.00		
	2	9.00		
	3	12.00	8.75	9.00
	4	8.00	9.25	9.81
2012	1	8.00	10.38	11.00
	2	13.50	11.63	12.25
	3	17.00	12.88	13.38
	4	13.00	13.88	14.72
2013	1	12.00	15.56	17.19
	2	20.25	18.81	19.63
	3	30.00	20.44	21.19
	4	19.50	21.94	
2014	1	18.00		

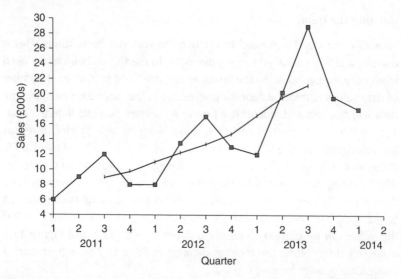

Figure 11.4 Time series graph of sun cream sales with the moving averages plotted

Isolating the seasonal component

There are two models that will allow you to isolate the seasonal component. The first is the *additive* model and is applicable if the seasonal swings are a constant difference from the trend. This means that the difference between the trend and a particular period remains approximately constant throughout the entire time series. The second model is the *multiplicative* model and is applicable if the seasonal swings are a constant percentage of the trend; that is, the seasonal swing will depend on the value of the trend at that point. In equation form the additive model is:

$$Y = T + S + C + R$$

and the multiplicative model is:

$$Y = T \times S \times C \times R$$

where Y is the variable of interest, T is the trend, S is the seasonal component, C is the cyclic component and R is the random element.

Although in many cases it is obvious which model is applicable in some cases it is not clear cut and both models should be tried to find out which gives the lowest errors. In the sales of sun cream it looks as if the sales are increasing relative to the trend so a multiplicative model will probably be the most appropriate model. However both models will be used in order to demonstrate the technique.

Additive model

To obtain the seasonal differences, the additive model can be rearranged as:

$$S + C + R = Y - T$$

So the value of the variable minus the trend value at that point will give you the seasonal difference plus the cyclic and random components. The cyclic component can only be isolated when values of the variable Y are available over many years (at least 20), which is rare. Usually the cyclic component is ignored, and its effect (if any) forms part of the random element.

For quarter 3 of 2011 the estimate of the seasonal difference is $12 - 9 = 3$. This tells you that sales for quarter 3 in 2011 are 3 units (£3000) above the trend. For quarter 4 of 2011 the seasonal difference is –1.81 (8 – 9.81), which means the sales are 1.81 below the trend. The seasonal difference for the entire series can be seen in Table 11.3.

If you look at these figures you will notice that for the same quarter number the seasonal difference varies. This is due to the random element. This variation can best be observed in Table 11.4, which also allows the average seasonal difference to be calculated.

The use of an average value helps to remove some of the random component. These averages should sum to zero since they should cancel out over the year. In the example above the sum of the averages is 0.222 and each average needs to be reduced by 0.056 (0.222/4) in order to ensure this condition.

Table 11.3 Seasonal differences for the sales of sun cream

Year	Quarter	Sales £000s)	Centered moving average	Seasonal difference
2011	1	6.00		
	2	9.00		
	3	12.00	9.00	3.00
	4	8.00	9.81	−1.81
2012	1	8.00	11.00	−3.00
	2	13.50	12.25	1.25
	3	17.00	13.38	3.63
	4	13.00	14.72	−1.72
2013	1	12.00	17.19	−5.19
	2	20.25	19.63	0.62
	3	30.00	21.19	8.81
	4	19.50		
2014	1	18.00		

Table 11.4 Average seasonal differences for the sales of sun cream

Quarter	1	2	3	4	
2011			3.00	−1.81	
2012	−3.00	1.25	3.63	−1.72	
2013	−5.19	0.62	8.81		
Average	−4.095	0.935	5.147	−1.765	Sum = 0.222
Adjusted	−4.15	0.88	5.09	−1.82	Sum = 0.00

Multiplicative model

The calculations for the multiplicative model are similar except that S is called the seasonal factor and is worked out by dividing Y by T. These factors are often expressed in percentage form by multiplying by 100. For example, the seasonal factor for quarter 3 in 2011 is $\frac{12}{9} \times 100 = 133.3\%$. This means that quarter 3 2011 is 133% of the current trend value. A value above 100% represents sales above the trend and a value below 100% represents sales below the trend. All the seasonal factors can be seen in Table 11.5 while Table 11.6 gives the average season factors. Each average was adjusted by 1.00781 (400/396.9) since the sum of the averages should in this case be 400.

Analysis of errors

Once you have isolated the trend and seasonal components it is a good idea to see how well the model fits the data. This is particularly important when

Table 11.5 Seasonal factors for the sales of sun cream

Year	Quarter	Sales £000s)	Centered moving average	Seasonal factor %
2011	1	6.00		
	2	9.00		
	3	12.00	9.00	133.3
	4	8.00	9.81	81.5
2012	1	8.00	11.00	72.7
	2	13.50	12.25	110.2
	3	17.00	13.38	127.1
	4	13.00	14.72	88.3
2013	1	12.00	17.19	69.8
	2	20.25	19.63	103.2
	3	30.00	21.19	141.6
	4	19.50		
2014	1	18.00		

Table 11.6 Calculation of the average seasonal factors for the sales of sun cream

Quarter	1	2	3	4	
2011			133.3	81.5	
2012	72.7	110.2	127.1	88.3	
2013	69.8	103.2	141.6		
Average	71.3	106.7	134.0	84.9	Sum = 396.9
Adjusted	71.9	107.5	135.0	85.6	Sum = 400.0

you are not sure whether the additive or multiplicative model is the correct model to use.

For the additive model $Y = T + S$, so the Y variable can be predicted by adding the trend to the relevant adjusted average seasonal difference. For the multiplicative model $Y = T \times S$, so the prediction is made by multiplying the trend and adjusted average seasonal factor. In both cases the difference between the actual value and the predicted value gives you the error in the prediction. For example, the predicted sales of sun cream for quarter 3 in 2011 using the additive model is $9.00 + 5.09 = 14.09$. Since the actual value is 12.00, this represents an error of -2.09 ($12 - 14.09$). Using the multiplicative model the predicted value is $9 \times \dfrac{135.0}{100} = 12.15$ so the error in this case is -0.15 ($12 - 12.15$). The errors for both models are shown in Tables 11.7 and 11.8.

Table 11.7   Calculation of the errors for the additive model

Year	Quarter	Sales £000s)	Trend	Average seasonal difference	Predicted sales (£000s)	Error	Squared error
2011	1	6.00					
	2	9.00					
	3	12.00	9.00	5.09	14.09	−2.09	4.3681
	4	8.00	9.81	−1.82	7.99	0.01	0.0001
2012	1	8.00	11.00	−4.15	6.85	1.15	1.3225
	2	13.50	12.25	0.88	13.13	0.37	0.1369
	3	17.00	13.38	5.09	18.47	−1.47	2.1609
	4	13.00	14.72	−1.82	12.90	0.10	0.0100
2013	1	12.00	17.19	−4.15	13.04	−1.04	1.0816
	2	20.25	19.63	0.88	20.51	−0.25	0.0676
	3	30.00	21.19	5.09	26.28	3.72	13.8384
	4	19.50				Sum	22.9861
2014	1	18.00				Mean	2.5540

Table 11.8 Calculation of the errors for the multiplicative model

Year	Quarter	Sales £000s)	Trend	Average seasonal factor (%)	Predicted sales (£000s)	Error	Squared error
2011	1	6.00					
	2	9.00					
	3	12.00	9.00	135.0	12.15	−0.15	0.0225
	4	8.00	9.81	85.6	8.40	−0.40	0.1600
2012	1	8.00	11.00	71.9	7.91	0.09	0.0081
	2	13.50	12.25	107.5	13.17	0.33	0.1089
	3	17.00	13.38	135.0	18.06	−1.06	1.1236
	4	13.00	14.72	85.6	12.60	0.40	0.1600
2013	1	12.00	17.19	71.9	12.36	−0.36	0.1296
	2	20.25	19.63	107.5	21.10	−0.85	0.7225
	3	30.00	21.19	135.0	28.60	1.40	1.9321
	4	19.50				Sum	4.3673
2014	1	18.00				Mean	0.4853

In order to compare these errors of both models it is normal to calculate the *mean square error* (MSE). To do this each error is squared and the mean found. These calculations have been included in Tables 11.7 and 11.8 above. So for the additive model the MSE is 2.55 and for the multiplicative model it is 0.49. This confirms that the multiplicative model is the best one to use.

Forecasting using the decomposition model

One purpose of time series analysis is to use the results to forecast future values of the series. The procedure for this is to extrapolate the trend into the future and then apply the seasonal component to the forecast trend. There are various methods of extrapolating the trend. The simplest is to extrapolate by eye ('eyeballing') since other factors can then be considered, if necessary. For the sun cream example, a possible extrapolation of the trend has been made and can be seen in Figure 11.5.

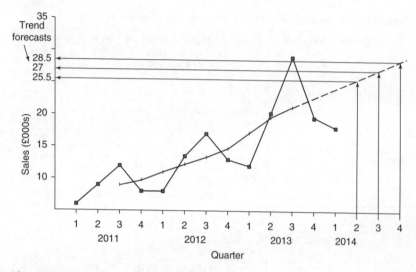

Figure 11.5 Trend forecasts for sales of sun cream

The forecast trend values for the remainder of 2014 have been read off this graph and are shown below:

Quarter	2	3	4
Trend forecast	25.5	27.0	28.5

To calculate the forecast for each quarter using the multiplicative model, these trend forecasts need to be multiplied by the appropriate seasonal factor. For example, for quarter 2 the average seasonal factor is 107.5%, so the forecast value is

$25.5 \times 1.075 = 27.41$, or approximately £27 400. However, any forecasts are subject to considerable uncertainty and all forecasts should be treated with caution.

Exponential smoothing

The technique of exponential smoothing is often used where a short-term forecast is required (that is, the next period). The formula for this technique is very simple:

Next forecast = Last forecast + $\alpha \times$ error in last forecast

where α (alpha) is a smoothing constant. This constant takes a value between 0 and 1, so that the next forecast will simply be the last forecast plus a fraction of the last error. The error in the last forecast is the actual value minus the forecast.

Example 11.2

Imagine that you are responsible for ensuring that the Small Brewery Company has sufficient barrels available to store its beer. Full barrels are sent out and empty ones returned. You need to know how many barrels will be returned the next day to plan production. If insufficient barrels are available, beer is wasted, whereas if more barrels than expected are returned, you may have lost sales.

There are two problems with exponential smoothing. The first is what value of α to use. This can only be found by trial and error, and you may even have to change the value in the light of experience. It is usually found that a value between 0.05 and 0.3 gives the smallest values of MSE. For the Small Brewery Company, a value of 0.1 has been chosen.

The second problem is how to get the first forecast, since a last forecast is required. Some people choose a suitable value while others prefer a warm-up period. Once several forecasts have been made, the starting value becomes less important anyway, but let us suppose that you have decided to use the warm-up method. You are to use the last 10 days for this purpose, and therefore your first proper forecast will be for day 11. The number of barrels returned over the last 10 days are:

Day	1	2	3	4	5	6	7	8	9	10
No. of barrels	20	13	19	19	25	17	15	13	22	20

If you take the forecast for day 2 as the actual for day 1, then the error is −7 (13 − 20)

and the forecast for day 3 becomes:

$$20 + (0.1 \times -7) = 19.3$$

The forecast for day 4 is now:

$$19.3 + (0.1 \times -0.3) = 19.27 \text{ and so on.}$$

This process has been continued in Table 11.9.

The time series of the original data and of the forecast values are shown in Figure 11.6. Also shown is the forecast using an α of 0.5, and you will see that a value of 0.1 gives a smoother series. This is generally true: the smaller the value of α, the greater the smoothing effect. In terms of accuracy the errors can again be analysed and MSE calculated. Using an α of 0.1, an MSE of 17.97 is obtained. For an α of 0.5 the MSE is 23.21.

Simple exponential smoothing is a very useful and easy-to-use short-term forecasting technique. However, it will lag behind a series that is undergoing a sharp change, such as a series that has a seasonal component or a steep trend. If you want to use it on seasonal data you must either seasonally

Table 11.9 Forecasts using exponential smoothing and a smoothing constant of 0.1

Day	No. barrels	Forecast	Error	a x error	Next forecast
1	20				
2	13	20.00	−7.00	−0.70	19.30
3	19	19.30	−0.30	−0.03	19.27
4	19	19.27	−0.27	−0.03	19.24
5	25	19.24	5.76	0.58	19.82
6	17	19.82	−2.82	−0.28	19.54
7	15	19.54	−4.54	−0.45	19.09
8	13	19.09	−6.09	−0.61	18.48
9	22	18.48	3.52	0.35	18.83
10	20	18.83	1.17	0.12	18.95
11		18.95			

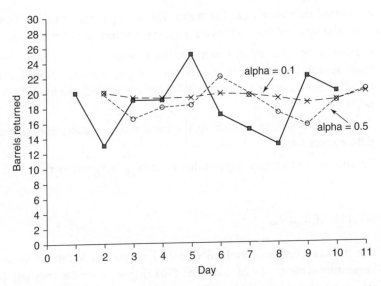

Figure 11.6 Numbers of returned barrels and forecasts using exponential smoothing

adjust the series first or use a more complex model such as the *Holt Winter's* model. Details of this model can be found in the further reading section at the end of this chapter.

KEY POINTS

* A time series can consist of a seasonal component, a trend, a long-term cycle and randomness. Unless we have over 20 years of data we normally ignore the long-term cycle.
* To isolate the trend of a time series we use the technique of moving averages.
* To isolate the seasonality we can either use the additive or multiplicative models. The additive model is used when the seasonal fluctuations are

a constant difference from the trend. The multiplicative model is used when the seasonal fluctuations are a constant proportion of the trend.

★ We can sometimes tell by looking at the time series chart which is the most appropriate model to use. If not, we can use both models and calculate the mean square error (MSE). The model with the lowest MSE is the best.

★ To obtain forecasts we extrapolate the trend and then apply the seasonal difference or factor.

★ For short-term forecasts, exponential smoothing is a good method.

FURTHER READING

This chapter is only an introduction to the huge subject of time series and forecasting. Chapter 13 of Oakshott (2012) gives a similar coverage to this text and also explains how Excel can be used to help in the analysis. There are a large number of more advanced models that can be used. If you have an interest in the subject and are good at maths then the text by Makridakis et al. (1998) gives a thorough coverage but is quite technical. Forecasting techniques are used in sports and the text by Eastaway and Haigh (2011) is worth reading. The Operational Research (OR) Society has published an article on 50 years of OR in sport (Wright, 2009) and part of this publication discusses forecasting models used in sport.

REVISION QUESTIONS

1 The personnel department of BBS plc, a large food processing company, is concerned about absenteeism among its shop floor workforce. There is a general feeling that the underlying trend has been rising, but nobody has yet analysed the figures. The total number of shop floor employees has remained virtually unchanged over the last few years.

The mean number of absentees per day is given below for each quarter of the years 2011 to 2013 and quarter 1 of 2014.

	Q1	Q2	Q3	Q4
2011	25.1	14.4	9.5	23.7
2012	27.9	16.9	12.4	26.1
2013	31.4	19.7	15.9	29.9
2014	34.5			

(a) Plot the data on a graph (leave space for the remaining 2014 figures).

(b) Use the method of moving averages to determine the trend in the series and superimpose this on your graph. Interpret your graph.

(c) Use an appropriate method to measure the seasonal pattern in the data.

Briefly give reasons for your choice of method.

(d) Use your analysis to produce rough forecasts of the mean number of absentees there will be in the remaining quarters of 2014.

2 The manager of the electrical department at a high street store has asked you to perform a time series analysis on the quarterly sales figures of the numbers of TVs sold over the past 3 years (see below).

Year	Quarter	No. of sales
2011	2	100
	3	125
	4	127
2012	1	102
	2	104
	3	128
	4	130
2013	1	107
	2	110
	3	131
	4	133
2014	1	107

(a) Produce a line graph of the number of sales. (Extend your time axes up to quarter 4 of 2014.) Describe the pattern exhibited by the data.

(b) Use moving averages to calculate the trend in your data and add this to your chart.

(c) What would be the best decomposition model, the additive or multiplicative? (Hint – calculate the MSE statistic for both models.)

(d) Extrapolate the trend and using your chosen model forecast the sales for the rest of 2014.

3 The following data refers to the daily end-of-business share prices (in pence) for a particular company:

112, 111, 113, 115, 114, 112, 115, 111, 111, 112, 113

Use exponential smoothing with a smoothing constant of 0.1 to forecast the price on day 12.

12
LINEAR PROGRAMMING

OBJECTIVES

- To be able to formulate linear programming models for both maximizing and minimizing problems
- To know how to apply a graphical method to solve two-variable problems
- To understand the concept of shadow prices, and to be able to calculate their value.
- To be able to carry out a sensitivity analysis on the problem

INTRODUCTION

Industry, and business in general, operates with limited resources. Frequently money, material and space are scarce, and companies attempt to utilize their resources as efficiently as is possible. The technique of linear programming is a procedure that can provide the best solution to many problems that involve an objective, such as profit maximization, and a series of linear constraints, such as time, labour and cost. This chapter introduces the technique and applies it to simple problems that can be solved graphically.

Optimizing the Timetable of the Mobile Library Service on the Isle of Wight

Most towns in the UK have a library, but for many people who live in the countryside it is not always easy or possible to get to visit the library. To overcome this problem many local authorities provide a mobile library service which visits set areas on a regular basis. The Isle of Wight, a small island off the south coast of England, provides this service. However, with the recent reduction in grants from central government to local authorities, they are looking at ways to continue to provide a high-quality service but at a reduced cost. As most of the cost is a made up of vehicles and drivers, a reduction in total mileage and time spent on the routes would make significant savings.

Currently the service serves 98 locations over a 16-day schedule. A total of 282.5 miles is driven over this period and the total driving time amounts to 35.5 hours.

This is a routing problem and the *Travelling Salesman Problem* is one well-known member of this class of problems. In this problem the objective is to find the lowest cost tour so that a number of nodes (e.g. cities) are visited exactly once before returning to the 'home' node. To solve this type of problem a form of linear programming model is used called *mixed integer linear programming* model. By applying this model a total driving time of 26.65 hours was obtained giving a saving of 8.85 hours or almost 25%. This is a significant saving and will reduce the cost of providing the service. A summary of the existing and amended daily driving times is shown in Table 12.1. The standard deviation is a measure of how the driving times vary from day to day. As can be seen the proposed timetable also has a smaller value of this statistic.

Table 12.1 Summary of driving times for current and proposed timetable

	Current timetable	Proposed timetable
Total driving time	35.5 hours	26.65 hours
Standard deviation	38 minutes	32 minutes

Source: T. Rienthonga, A. Walker and T. Bektas (2011) Look, here comes the library van! Optimizing the timetable of the mobile library service on the Isle of Wight. OR Insight vol 24, 1, 49–62

BASICS OF LINEAR PROGRAMMING

Linear programming (or LP) is concerned with the management of scarce resources. It is particularly applicable where two or more activities are competing for these limited resources. For example, a company might want to make several different products, each of which makes different demands on the limited resources available. How many of each product should be made so that contribution to profits is maximized? Or perhaps you want to determine the quantities of raw materials necessary for a particular blend of oil that will minimize the cost of production.

Before these and other problems can be solved you have to formulate the problem in linear programming terms. This involves expressing the problem as a series of inequations and finding solutions to these inequations that optimize some objective. This may sound very difficult, but for two-variable problems (for example, two products) the problem can be solved using a graphical technique. For larger problems computer software is normally used.

MODEL FORMULATION

Before a problem can be solved by the linear programming method, a model needs to be developed. The model consists of a description of the problem in mathematical terms. In particular, the variables of the problem need to be defined and the objective decided. In addition, the constraints need to be expressed as inequations.

The procedure will be explained using the following example.

Example 12.1

The company Just Shirts has been formed to make high-quality shirts and is planning to make two types – the 'Regular Fit' and the 'Deluxe Fit'. The contribution to profits for each shirt is £5 for each Regular Fit shirt made and £8 for each Deluxe Fit shirt. To make each shirt requires cotton, of which 600 square metres is available each day, and machinists to cut and stitch the shirts. Twenty machinists are employed by the company and they each work an 8-hour day, giving 160 hours of labour in total. Each Regular Fit shirt requires 5 square metres of cotton and takes 1 hour to make, while each Deluxe Fit shirt takes 6 square metres of cotton and 2 hours to make. The company wishes to maximize contribution to profits, so how many of each type of shirt should be made on a daily basis?

In order to represent the problem in mathematical terms we need to use variables to represent the products. So Let R represent the number of Regular Fit shirts that are to be made each day and D represent the number of Deluxe Fit shirts.

Our objective is to maximize profits so this can be written as:

Max. $5R + 8D$

As the profit on regular shirts is £5 and Deluxe shirts £8

We now need to set up the constraints

If you make R Regular Fit shirts then you will use $5R$ metres of cotton. Similarly you will use $6D$ metres of cotton to make D Deluxe Fit shirts. The sum of these two must be less than or equal to 600 square metres, so this can be written as:

$5R + 6D \leq 600$

Similarly for the labour resource we have:

$R + 2D \leq 160$

We should also indicate that we are only interested in positive values of R and D, so these non-negativity constraints are written as $R \geq 0$ and $D \geq 0$

To summarize the LP formulation for this problem is:

Max. $5R + 8D$

Subject to:

$5R + 6D \leq 600$

$R + 2D \leq 160$

$R, D \geq 0$

There are many values of R and D that will satisfy these inequations. For instance, $R = 40$ and $D = 20$ would satisfy all the constraints, so this is a feasible combination. The problem is, which combination will give the largest profit?

GRAPHICAL SOLUTION OF LINEAR PROGRAMMING PROBLEMS

The formulation of the problem is only the start (but for many students the hardest part). You now have to solve the problem. *Solver* an Excel add-on will solve LP problems, but for two-variable problems it is possible to solve the problem graphically.

If, for the moment, you replace the inequality signs by equalities, the two main constraints become:

$5R + 6D = 600$

and

$$R + 2D = 160$$

Since these equations contain only two variables, R and D, they can be represented as straight lines and plotted on a graph. Two points are required to plot a straight line and it is convenient to find where they cross the axes. To do this it is simply a matter of letting $R = 0$ and calculating D, and then letting $D = 0$ and calculating R.

The points where the two lines cross the axes are summarized in Table 12.2. These two lines have been plotted on a graph (see Figure 12.1) and they mark the boundaries of the inequations.

Table 12.2 Crossing points for the two constraints

Constraint	R	D
Cotton	0	100
	120	0
	0	80
Labour	160	0

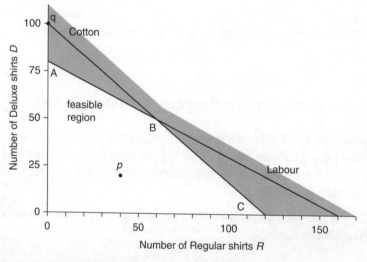

Figure 12.1 Graphical solution for the Just Shirts problem

The region satisfying each inequation will be one side of the boundary. In this example the regions for both inequations are below the lines. To identify the required region it is normal to shade the unwanted region; that is, the region not satisfying the inequality. The region that satisfies all inequalities is called the *feasible* region: any point within this region will satisfy all the constraints. From the graph for the Just Shirts example you should be able to identify the feasible region as 0ABC.

Any point within the feasible region will satisfy all constraints, but which point or points give the largest profit? Fortunately it can be shown that the optimum point is always at a corner point of the feasible region. The corner points for this problem have been labelled in Figure 12.1 using the letters A, B and C. The values of R and D are shown in Table 12.3.

As point B gives the largest profit this is the optimum point so 60 regular shirts and 50 deluxe shirts should be made.

Table 12.3 Profit at each corner point of the feasible region

	R	D	Profit
Point A	0	80	£640
Point B	60	50	£700
Point C	120	0	£600

TIGHT AND SLACK CONSTRAINTS

If you substitute the optimal values of R (60) and D (50) back into the constraints you will get the following:

Cotton: $5 \times 60 + 6 \times 50 = 600$
Labour: $60 + 2 \times 50 = 160$

Since these values correspond to the maximum quantity of both resources available, the resources are *scarce* and are called *tight* or *binding* constraints. Where a constraint has not reached its limit it is referred to as a *slack* or *non-binding* constraint.

By increasing the right-hand side of a tight constraint you will find that the profit will increase. For example if you could get another 10 m² of cotton the cotton constraint would become:

$$5R + 6D = 610$$

If you redraw the graph or solve the two constraints using algebra (simultaneous equations) you will find that the values of R and D have changed to $R = 65$, $D = 47.5$ giving a profit of £705. This is an increase of £5. The increase in profit for every unit increase in a tight resource is called the *shadow price* of that resource and in this case it will be 5/10 = £0.50. If you repeat the analysis for the labour constraint you will find that the shadow price for this resource is £2.50.

When you increase the right-hand side of a constraint what you are effectively doing is moving the boundary of the feasible region *away* from the origin. This can continue until that resource ceases to be scarce. In the case of the labour constraint it will cease to be a scarce when it reaches point q in Figure 12.1. At this point, $R = 0$ and $D = 100$ and if you substitute these values into the labour constraint you will get:

$$0 + 2 \times 100 = 200$$

So the labour resource can increase by 40 hours which means that a possible $40 \times 2.50 = £100$ extra profit can be made each day. Similarly the cotton constraint can be increased by 200 m² to a maximum of 800 m². This is left as an exercise for the reader (see question 3 in the revision section).

MINIMIZATION PROBLEMS

The Just Shirts example was a maximization problem because a solution was required that maximized the contribution to profits. However, equally important are minimization problems in which some objective, for example cost, is to be minimized. The general procedure for dealing with minimization problems is no different from maximization problems. A feasible region will still be obtained, but instead of finding the corner point of the feasible region that gives the largest value you are looking for the point that gives the smallest value. All minimization problems must have at least one 'greater than or equal to' constraint, otherwise the origin (0,0) will be the optimum point.

Example 12.2

Ratkins, a local DIY store, has decided to advertise on television and radio but is unsure about the number of adverts it should place. It wishes to minimize the total cost of the campaign and has limited the total number of 'slots' to no more than 5. However, it wants to have at least one slot on both media. The company has been told that one TV slot will be seen by 1 million viewers, while a slot on local radio will only be heard by 100 000 listeners. The company wishes to reach an audience of at least 2 million people. If the cost of advertising is £5000 for each radio slot and £20 000 for each TV slot, how should it advertise?

This problem can be solved by the graphical method of linear programming because there are two variables: the number of radio adverts and the number of TV adverts. The formulation for this problem is as follows:

Let $R =$ no. of radio adverts and $T =$ no. of TV adverts:

$$\text{Min. } 5000R = 20000T$$

Subject to:

$$0.1R + T \geq 2 \quad \text{(Minimum audience in millions)}$$
$$R + T \leq 5 \quad \text{(Maximum number of 'slots')}$$
$$R \geq 1 \quad \text{(At least one radio slot)}$$
$$T \geq 1 \quad \text{(At least on TV slot)}$$

The procedure for drawing the graph is the same as that for the maximizing case. That is, it is necessary to find the points at which the constraints cut the axes. Table 12.4 gives these values.

Table 12.4 Crossing points for Example 12.2

Constraint	R	T
Audience	20	2
Total slots	5	5
Min. slots for radio	1	—
Min. slots for TV	—	1

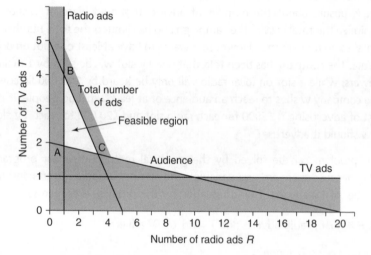

Figure 12.2 Graphical solution for the advertising problem (Example 12.2)

The graph for this problem is shown in Figure 12.2. The feasible region is given by the area enclosed by ABC. The optimum point will be at one of these corners, and this time it is necessary to find the point that gives the *minimum* value. You should find that the coordinates and hence the cost at each of the corner points are as given in Table 12.5.

Point A gives the minimum cost of £43 000. This solution implies that the company should buy 1 radio advert and 1.9 TV adverts, hardly a sensible solution. Unfortunately, linear programming will give fractional values, and if this is not sensible *integer linear programming* should be used. This

Table 12.5 Solution to Example 12.2

	R	T	Cost
A	1	1.9	£43 000
B	1	4	£85 000
C	3.33	1.67	£50 050

technique is not covered in this book, but for two variable problems a more realistic solution can often be found by inspecting the graph. In this particular case it is simply a matter of rounding the 1.9 to 2, which increases the cost to £45 000. However, do take care as rounding can often give you an infeasible solution. This can be avoided by checking to see that all constraints are still satisfied. In this example R = 1 and T = 2 does satisfy all 4 constraints.

KEY POINTS

★ Linear programming is a method that finds the best solution amongst many possible solutions. It is an optimizing technique.

★ The method requires an objective function, which can be either maximize or minimize, and a set of linear constraints.

★ For two variable problems a graphical method can be used.

★ The shadow price of a resource is the resulting change in the objective function when the right-hand side of a resource is changed by one unit.

FURTHER READING

Linear programming is an operational research (OR) technique and any text with OR or management science in the title will almost certainly include this technique. Chapter 14 in Oakshott (2012) extends the ideas presented in this text and includes some details of solving LP problems using Solver. There is quite a lot of maths involved in the LP algorithm, but fortunately it is not necessary for the business student to know details of how the algorithm works. In fact most students think that formulating the problem already contains too much maths! However, for the student who wants to find out more about this important technique the book by Anderson et al. (2008) is a good choice.

REVISION QUESTIONS

1   A manufacturer produces two products, P and Q, which when sold earn contributions of £600 and £400 per unit, respectively. The manufacture of each product requires time on a lathe and a polishing machine. Each unit of P requires 2 hours on the lathe and 1 hour on the polishing machine, while Q requires 1 hour on each machine. Each day, 10 hours are available on the lathe and 7 hours on the polishing machine. Determine the number of units of P and Q that should be produced per day to maximize contribution.

2   A company is planning a radio and TV advertising campaign and it has decided that it must use at least 60 adverts, have no more than 50 radio adverts, have at least as many radio as TV adverts and not exceed a budget of £34 000.

   A radio advert is not as effective as a TV advertisement and the industry assigns a rating to each of the media to indicate their relative effectiveness. For radio the rating is 200 whereas TV gives a rating of 600.
   (a) Assuming it is required to maximize the ratings, use the graphical technique of linear programming to find the number of each type of advertisement.
   (b) What constraints are binding? What would happen to the overall rating if the maximum number of radio advertisements was increased to 100?

3   In Example 12.1 (page 204) prove that the cotton constraint can be increased by 200 m^2 to a maximum of 800 m^2. What is the increase in profit?

4 A wealthy investor has £550 000 in a bank account that she wishes to invest and is considering four general types of investment, which are: Government bonds, Corporate bonds, FTSE 100 stocks, and Aim stocks

The goal of the investor is to maximize the rate of return on the money invested, where the annual expected return for each investment type is 4%, 5%, 6% and 8%, respectively. Any money not invested in one of these investment type remains in the bank where it earns interest at 3%.

The investor has decided to invest at least £50 000 on corporate bonds and that no more than £300 000 will be put into investments with an element of risk (i.e. corporate bonds and stocks). In addition she decides that at least one half of the money invested in the above 4 ways will go into stocks. Also no more than 25% of the money invested will go into the very risky Aim stocks.

(a) Formulate this problem as a four-variable linear programming problem

13

CRITICAL PATH ANALYSIS

OBJECTIVES

- To know how to construct an activity-on-node network to represent a project
- To be able to calculate the earliest and latest start and finish times for each activity
- To be able to calculate the float for each activity, and to identify the critical path
- To know how to apply the technique of crashing

INTRODUCTION

Whenever a large or complex project is undertaken a great deal of planning is necessary. Building a house is a good example as there are many tasks or activities that have to be completed, some of which can proceed at the same time while others have to wait until preceding tasks are completed. The critical path analysis (CPA) method identifies the activities that must start on time and cannot be delayed. These *critical* activities form a path (or paths) through the network and the time taken to complete this path gives the minimum time for the project to be completed. There are two different approaches to obtaining the *critical path* and in this chapter we will use the activity-on-node method. We will also look at a method for reducing the time of a project using a technique called *crashing*.

Network Rail's Leven Viaduct

The Leven viaduct is a 49 span structure that crosses the Leven estuary and carries trains on the Barrow to Lancaster line. It was built in 1857 and then rebuilt in 1915, but no major repair work has been done on it since. The structure was falling into disrepair, and without major rebuilding it would have had to be closed and trains diverted onto the already congested West coast main line. In 2006 the decision was made to rebuild the viaduct at a cost of £14m.

A project of this magnitude requires careful planning. Some 3,500 tonnes of steelwork had to be produced, 1,100 metres of track had to be replaced and 2000 m^2 of brickwork repairs were required. In all hundreds of separate processes were involved; some that could be done in parallel while others were dependent on the completion of preceding activities. A general plan of operations is as follows.

- Carry out survey
- Create design
- Steelwork fabrication
- Prepare site Construction work

Some of the work such as steelwork fabrication could be done off-site, but once construction work is started the line cannot be used. It was therefore important to ensure that this time was kept to a minimum.

On 16 July 2006 the viaduct was officially reopened after only 16 weeks closure. In February 2007 the project won a prestigious engineering award. The structure is now good for another 150 years!

Source: Times 100 Case Studies, Business Case Studies LLP

THE ACTIVITY–ON–NODE METHOD

This technique allows the time of the project and the slack (or *float*) of individual activities to be determined. If an activity has zero float you would say that it is *critical* because any delay in that activity would delay the entire project.

Before critical path analysis (or CPA) is used it is necessary to make a list of all the activities, their durations and which activities must immediately precede them. Once this list has been completed, you should represent the project by the means of a diagram. The diagram used in this book uses the activity-on-node method. The basic diagram for this method is shown in Figure 13.1. The nodes represent the activity, and the lines the dependencies between activities.

Example 13.1

You have just obtained planning permission to build a garage and you are now in the process of planning the project. With a little help from a friendly builder you have made a list of activities that need to be completed, the durations of these activities and the order in which they can be tackled. This list is shown in Table 13.1.

The basic diagram for the garage problem is shown in Figure 13.2. You will see that the name of each activity is displayed in the box together with the duration. You will also see that there are start and end nodes. This is to ensure that every activity has at least one line entering and one line leaving its node.

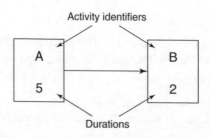

Figure 13.1 Activity-on-node

Table 13.1 Details of the garage building project

Activity	Description	Immediate preceding activities	Duration (days)
A	Obtain bricklayer	–	10
B	Dig the foundations	–	8
C	Lay the base	B	1
D	Build the walls	A and C	8
E	Build the roof	D	3
F	Tile the roof	E	2
G	Make window frames	–	3
H	Fit the window frames	D and G	1
I	Fit glass to frames	H	1
J	Fit the door	E	1
K	Paint the door and window frames	I and J	2
L	Point the brickwork	D	2

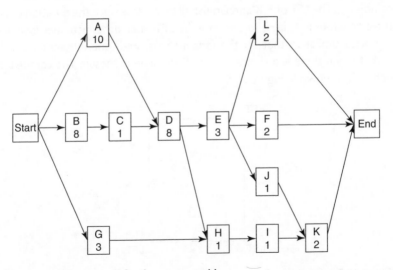

Figure 13.2 The network for the garage problem

For this method you need to display 4 additional pieces of information on each node: the earliest start time of the activity (EST), the latest start time (LST), the earliest finish time (EFT) and the latest finish time (LFT). This information should be displayed as in Figure 13.3.

In order to calculate the EST and EFT a *forward pass* is made through the network. If the start is at time zero, then the EST of activities A, B and G is zero and their EFT is 10, 8 and 3, respectively. The EST of activity C must be 8, since it can start as soon as B is completed. However, what about activity D? This activity cannot start until both A and C are completed, and as A is completed later than C, then activity A determines the EST of D, which must be 10. This is the general rule when calculating the EST – if there are two or more choices the EST is the *larger* of the EFTs of the preceding activities. From this you will see that the EST of K must be 22 and not 20. If this process is continued you will end up with the EST and EFT values shown in Figure 13.4 where you can see that the project will take 24 days in total.

To enable the LFT and LST to be calculated a *backward pass* is made through the network, starting at the END node. The LFT of activities F, K and L must be 24 since the project is only complete when all these activities have been completed. The LST of F, K and L must all be 22 days since the duration of all three activities is 2 days. To calculate the LFT of all other activities involves a process similar to that for the forward pass, with one difference, which is that when there is a choice, the *smallest* value is chosen. The completed network is shown in Figure 13.5.

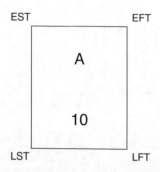

Figure 13.3 Information displayed on each node

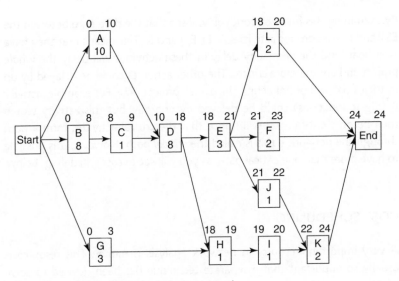

Figure 13.4 A forward pass through the network

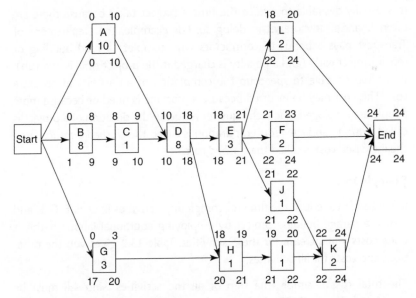

Figure 13.5 The completed network

By examining this final network you will see that the difference between the EST and LST is zero for activities A, D, E, J and K. This means that they have zero float, and therefore, any delay in these activities will delay the whole project and are therefore *critical*. The other activities could be delayed by up to their float without affecting the overall project time. For example, activity B (dig foundations) could be delayed by one day, but this activity would then become critical. You will notice that the critical activities form a path through the network – this is called the *critical path*. However, it is possible to have more than one critical path, as you will see in cost scheduling, below.

COST SCHEDULING

A very important resource in network analysis is money. This resource is usually so important that a separate technique has been devised to solve problems posed by financial considerations. This technique is called *crashing*.

It is usually desirable to reduce the time a project takes because there are often financial advantages in doing so. For example, the Department of Transport pays a bonus to contractors who complete a road building or repair project early (and a penalty is charged if the project time is overrun). It is often possible to speed up the completion of an activity at an extra cost. This cost may be incurred because a machine is hired or because more people are employed. The technique for reducing the duration of a project is called *crashing* and the reduced duration is called the *crashed duration*, and the increased cost is called the *crashed cost*.

Example 15.3

It is possible to reduce the time for completing activities B, D, E, F, G, K and L of the garage building project by employing additional labour. If this is done costs will increase for these activities. Table 13.2 gives you the durations and costs for all activities.

The total cost is simply the sum of all the activities, since all must be completed. This is £2175. If some of the activities are crashed this cost will increase. The question is: which activities should be crashed in order to

Table 13.2 Cost details for the garage project

Activity	Normal duration (days)	Crash duration (days)	Normal cost	Crash cost
A	10	10	£5	£5
B	8	2	£100	£700
C	1	1	£200	£200
D	8	5	£800	£1700
E	3	2	£500	£900
F	2	1	£200	£400
G	3	1	£150	£550
H	1	1	£50	£50
I	1	1	£20	£20
J	1	1	£20	£20
K	2	1	£30	£130
L	2	1	£100	£200

Table 13.3 Daily cost of crashing

Activity	Max. reduction by crashing (days)	Extra cost	Crash cost/Day
B	6	£600	£100
D	3	£900	£300
E	1	£400	£400
F	1	£200	£200
G	2	£400	£200
K	1	£100	£100
L	1	£100	£100

reduce the project time to a minimum but without incurring unnecessary costs? To help with this decision it is useful to find the crash cost per unit time (day in this example). Table 13.3 gives this information.

Since the critical path is the longest path through the network activities on this path should be crashed first. However by crashing the critical path it is likely that non-critical activities become critical so making other paths critical. To ensure that only critical activities are crashed it is useful to list all major paths through the network as has been done in Table 13.4.

Table 13.4 Paths through the network

Path	Duration
ADEJK	24
BCDEJK	23
ADEF	23
ADHIK	22
BCDEF	22
BCDHIK	21
ADL	20
BCDL	19

Table 13.5 Steps involved in crashing the network

Path	Duration	Step 1	Step 2	Step 3
ADEJK	24	23	20	19
BCDEJK	23	22	19	18
ADEF	23	23	20	19
ADHIK	22	21	18	18
BCDEF	22	22	19	18
BCDHIK	21	20	17	17
ADL	20	20	17	17
BCDL	19	19	16	16
Activities crashed		K – 1	D – 3	E – 1
Extra cost		£100	£900	£400
Cumulative extra cost		£100	£1000	£1400

Looking at Table 13.3 we see that activity K is the cheapest activity to crash and can be crashed by 1 day at a cost of £100. This reduces path ADEJK to 23 days which is the same as path ADEF and this means that we now have two critical paths. If we examine Table 13.3 we see that we can crash activities D, E and F. However D and E are common to both paths and since D is the cheapest we crash this by its maximum of 3 days. Finally we crash E by 1 day giving a final duration of 19 days. This process is summarized in Table 13.5.

In this example we have reduced the duration by 5 days at a cost of £1400. However, we have made activity F critical in the process.

KEY POINTS

★ Critical path analysis identifies the minimum time in which the project can be completed, together with the critical activities and the float of the non-critical activities.

★ The activity-on-node method can be used to draw the network so that these important results can be easily obtained.

★ In some cases the total duration of a project can be reduced by reducing the duration of individual activities. The technique of crashing allows this reduction to be carried out at minimum additional cost.

FURTHER READING

Most quantitative methods or management science texts include this topic. The one used here and also by Anderson et al. (2008) and Chapter 15 in Oakshott (2012) is the activity-on-node method. Some texts however such as Morris (2012) and Curwin and Slater (2008) use the activity-on-arrow method which is a slightly different way of portraying the network.

REVISION QUESTIONS

1 Yachtsteer manufactures a self-steering device for pleasure yachts and, as a result of increased competition from foreign manufacturers, it has decided to design and manufacture a new model in time for the next Boat Show. As a first step in planning the project, the major tasks and durations have been identified (Table 13.6). Draw a network to represent the logical sequence of tasks and determine how long it will be before the new product can be marketed.

2 Revor plc are urgently planning the production of their new lightweight car battery, the 'Epsilon'. They would like to exhibit their battery at a trade fair, which is to take place in 48 weeks' time. Various activities have to be completed before production can start, and these are shown in Table 13.7.

Table 13.6 Activities for Question 1

Task		Time (weeks)	Preceding tasks
A	Design new product	8	–
B	Design electronics	4	–
C	Organize production facilities	4	A
D	Obtain production materials	2	A
E	Manufacture trial gear	3	C,D
F	Obtain electronic circuit boards	2	B
G	Decide on yacht for trials	1	–
H	Assemble trial gear and electronics	2	E, F
I	Test product in workshops	3	H, G
J	Test product at sea	4	I
K	Assess product's performance	3	J
L	Plan national marketing	4	K

Table 13.7 Activities for Question 2

Tasks		Preceding tasks	Duration (weeks)
A	Clear area	–	20
B	Commission consulting engineers to design equipment	–	2
C	Receive consultant's report	B	10
D	Place equipment out to tender	C	1
E	Obtain equipment	D	6
F	Install equipment	A, E	30
G	Recruit additional staff	C	6
H	Train new staff	G	4
I	Order and obtain materials	–	16
J	Pilot production run	F, H, I	3
K	Advertise new product		2

(a) Draw the network and show that it is not possible to start production within 48 weeks. What are the critical activities and how much total float do the non-critical activities have?

(b) It is possible to 'crash' (i.e. reduce the duration of) certain activities at increased cost. These activities are shown in Table 13.8.

   (i) Ron Smith, the Production Manager, suggests that only activity I need be crashed because this is the cheapest option and allows the greatest reduction in time to be made. Explain why this would not help the situation.

   (ii) It has been estimated that for every week over 48 weeks that this project takes, a loss of £8000 is made as a result of lost profits. Decide on the strategy that will minimize the sum of crashed costs and loss of profits.

Table 13.8 Crash and cost details for Question 2

Activity	Crashed duration	Normal cost	Crashed cost (£000s)
A	18	4	10
E	5	1	3
F	28	15	27
I	8	0.5	8.5
J	2	16	26

APPENDIX 1
STATISTICAL TABLES

THE NORMAL TABLE

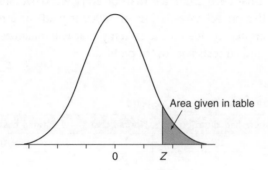

Figure A1.1 The standard normal distribution

Z	0.00	0.01	0.02	0.03	0.04	0.05	0.06	0.07	0.08	0.09
0.0	0.5000	0.4960	0.4920	0.4880	0.4840	0.4801	0.4761	0.4721	0.4681	0.4641
0.1	0.4602	0.4562	0.4522	0.4483	0.4443	0.4404	0.4364	0.4325	0.4286	0.4247
0.2	0.4207	0.4168	0.4129	0.4090	0.4052	0.4013	0.3974	0.3936	0.3897	0.3859
0.3	0.3821	0.3783	0.3745	0.3707	0.3669	0.3632	0.3594	0.3557	0.3520	0.3483
0.4	0.3446	0.3409	0.3372	0.3336	0.3300	0.3264	0.3228	0.3192	0.3156	0.3121
0.5	0.3085	0.3050	0.3015	0.2981	0.2946	0.2912	0.2877	0.2843	0.2810	0.2776
0.6	0.2743	0.2709	0.2676	0.2643	0.2611	0.2578	0.2546	0.2514	0.2483	0.2451
0.7	0.2420	0.2389	0.2358	0.2327	0.2296	0.2266	0.2236	0.2206	0.2177	0.2148
0.8	0.2119	0.2090	0.2061	0.2033	0.2005	0.1977	0.1949	0.1922	0.1894	0.1867
0.9	0.1841	0.1814	0.1788	0.1762	0.1736	0.1711	0.1685	0.1660	0.1635	0.1611
1.0	0.1587	0.1562	0.1539	0.1515	0.1492	0.1469	0.1446	0.1423	0.1401	0.1379

(continued)

Continued

Z	0.00	0.01	0.02	0.03	0.04	0.05	0.06	0.07	0.08	0.09
1.1	0.1357	0.1335	0.1314	0.1292	0.1271	0.1251	0.1230	0.1210	0.1190	0.1170
1.2	0.1151	0.1131	0.1112	0.1093	0.1075	0.1056	0.1038	0.1020	0.1003	0.0985
1.3	0.0968	0.0951	0.0934	0.0918	0.0901	0.0885	0.0869	0.0853	0.0838	0.0823
1.4	0.0808	0.0793	0.0778	0.0764	0.0749	0.0735	0.0721	0.0708	0.0694	0.0681
1.5	0.0668	0.0655	0.0643	0.0630	0.0618	0.0606	0.0594	0.0582	0.0571	0.0559
1.6	0.0548	0.0537	0.0526	0.0516	0.0505	0.0495	0.0485	0.0475	0.0465	0.0455
1.7	0.0446	0.0436	0.0427	0.0418	0.0409	0.0401	0.0392	0.0384	0.0375	0.0367
1.8	0.0359	0.0351	0.0344	0.0336	0.0329	0.0322	0.0314	0.0307	0.0301	0.0294
1.9	0.0287	0.0281	0.0274	0.0268	0.0262	0.0256	0.0250	0.0244	0.0239	0.0233
2.0	0.0228	0.0222	0.0217	0.0212	0.0207	0.0202	0.0197	0.0192	0.0188	0.0183
2.1	0.0179	0.0174	0.0170	0.0166	0.0162	0.0158	0.0154	0.0150	0.0146	0.0143
2.2	0.0139	0.0136	0.0132	0.0129	0.0125	0.0122	0.0119	0.0116	0.0113	0.0110
2.3	0.0107	0.0104	0.0102	0.0099	0.0096	0.0094	0.0091	0.0089	0.0087	0.0084
2.4	0.0082	0.0080	0.0078	0.0075	0.0073	0.0071	0.0069	0.0068	0.0066	0.0064
2.5	0.0062	0.0060	0.0059	0.0057	0.0055	0.0054	0.0052	0.0051	0.0049	0.0048
2.6	0.0047	0.0045	0.0044	0.0043	0.0041	0.0040	0.0039	0.0038	0.0037	0.0036
2.7	0.0035	0.0034	0.0033	0.0032	0.0031	0.0030	0.0029	0.0028	0.0027	0.0026
2.8	0.0026	0.0025	0.0024	0.0023	0.0023	0.0022	0.0021	0.0021	0.0020	0.0019
2.9	0.0019	0.0018	0.0018	0.0017	0.0016	0.0016	0.0015	0.0015	0.0014	0.0014
3.0	0.00135	3.1	0.000968	3.2	0.000687	3.3	0.000483	3.4	0.000337	

TABLE OF THE t-DISTRIBUTION

The table gives the t-value for a range of probabilities in the upper tail. For a two tailed test the probability should be halved.

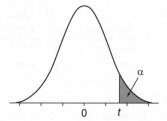

Figure A1.2 The t-distribution on v degrees of freedom

				Probability (α)				
v	0.2	0.1	0.05	0.025	0.01	0.005	0.001	0.0001
1	1.376	3.078	6.314	12.706	31.821	63.656	318.3	3185.3
2	1.061	1.886	2.920	4.303	6.965	9.925	22.328	70.706
3	0.978	1.638	2.353	3.182	4.541	5.841	10.214	22.203
4	0.941	1.533	2.132	2.776	3.747	4.604	7.173	13.039
5	0.920	1.476	2.015	2.571	3.365	4.032	5.894	9.676
6	0.906	1.440	1.943	2.447	3.143	3.707	5.208	8.023
7	0.896	1.415	1.895	2.365	2.998	3.499	4.785	7.064
8	0.889	1.397	1.860	2.306	2.896	3.355	4.501	6.442
9	0.883	1.383	1.833	2.262	2.821	3.250	4.297	6.009
10	0.879	1.372	1.812	2.228	2.764	3.169	4.144	5.694
11	0.876	1.363	1.796	2.201	2.718	3.106	4.025	5.453
12	0.873	1.356	1.782	2.179	2.681	3.055	3.930	5.263
13	0.870	1.350	1.771	2.160	2.650	3.012	3.852	5.111
14	0.868	1.345	1.761	2.145	2.624	2.977	3.787	4.985
15	0.866	1.341	1.753	2.131	2.602	2.947	3.733	4.880
16	0.865	1.337	1.746	2.120	2.583	2.921	3.686	4.790
17	0.863	1.333	1.740	2.110	2.567	2.898	3.646	4.715
18	0.862	1.330	1.734	2.101	2.552	2.878	3.610	4.648
19	0.861	1.328	1.729	2.093	2.539	2.861	3.579	4.590

(continued)

Continued

				Probability (α)				
ν	0.2	0.1	0.05	0.025	0.01	0.005	0.001	0.0001
20	0.860	1.325	1.725	2.086	2.528	2.845	3.552	4.539
21	0.859	1.323	1.721	2.080	2.518	2.831	3.527	4.492
22	0.858	1.321	1.717	2.074	2.508	2.819	3.505	4.452
23	0.858	1.319	1.714	2.069	2.500	2.807	3.485	4.416
24	0.857	1.318	1.711	2.064	2.492	2.797	3.467	4.382
25	0.856	1.316	1.708	2.060	2.485	2.787	3.450	4.352
26	0.856	1.315	1.706	2.056	2.479	2.779	3.435	4.324
27	0.855	1.314	1.703	2.052	2.473	2.771	3.421	4.299
28	0.855	1.313	1.701	2.048	2.467	2.763	3.408	4.276
29	0.854	1.311	1.699	2.045	2.462	2.756	3.396	4.254
30	0.854	1.310	1.697	2.042	2.457	2.750	3.385	4.234
35	0.852	1.306	1.690	2.030	2.438	2.724	3.340	4.153
40	0.851	1.303	1.684	2.021	2.423	2.704	3.307	4.094
45	0.850	1.301	1.679	2.014	2.412	2.690	3.281	4.049
50	0.849	1.299	1.676	2.009	2.403	2.678	3.261	4.014
60	0.848	1.296	1.671	2.000	2.390	2.660	3.232	3.962
80	0.846	1.292	1.664	1.990	2.374	2.639	3.195	3.899
100	0.845	1.290	1.660	1.984	2.364	2.626	3.174	3.861
∞	0.842	1.282	1.645	1.960	2.327	2.576	3.091	3.720

TABLE OF THE CHI−SQUARE DISTRIBUTION

This table gives chi-square values for a range of probabilities and degrees of freedom.

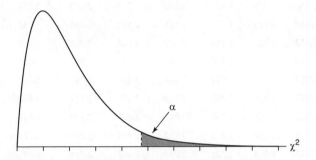

Figure A1.3 The chi-square distribution on v degrees of freedom

	Probability (α)								
v	0.995	0.99	0.9	0.1	0.05	0.025	0.01	0.005	0.001
1	0.000	0.000	0.016	2.706	3.841	5.024	6.635	7.879	10.827
2	0.010	0.020	0.211	4.605	5.991	7.378	9.210	10.597	13.815
3	0.072	0.115	0.584	6.251	7.815	9.348	11.345	12.838	16.266
4	0.207	0.297	1.064	7.779	9.488	11.143	13.277	14.860	18.466
5	0.412	0.554	1.610	9.236	11.070	12.832	15.086	16.750	20.515
6	0.676	0.872	2.204	10.645	12.592	14.449	16.812	18.548	22.457
7	0.989	1.239	2.833	12.017	14.067	16.013	18.475	20.278	24.321
8	1.344	1.647	3.490	13.362	15.507	17.535	20.090	21.955	26.124
9	1.735	2.088	4.168	14.684	16.919	19.023	21.666	23.589	27.877
10	2.156	2.558	4.865	15.987	18.307	20.483	23.209	25.188	29.588
11	2.603	3.053	5.578	17.275	19.675	21.920	24.725	26.757	31.264
12	3.074	3.571	6.304	18.549	21.026	23.337	26.217	28.300	32.909
13	3.565	4.107	7.041	19.812	22.362	24.736	27.688	29.819	34.527
14	4.075	4.660	7.790	21.064	23.685	26.119	29.141	31.319	36.124
15	4.601	5.229	8.547	22.307	24.996	27.488	30.578	32.801	37.698
16	5.142	5.812	9.312	23.542	26.296	28.845	32.000	34.267	39.252

(continued)

Continued

					Probability (α)				
ν	0.995	0.99	0.9	0.1	0.05	0.025	0.01	0.005	0.001
17	5.697	6.408	10.085	24.769	27.587	30.191	33.409	35.718	40.791
18	6.265	7.015	10.865	25.989	28.869	31.526	34.805	37.156	42.312
19	6.844	7.633	11.651	27.204	30.144	32.852	36.191	38.582	43.819
20	7.434	8.260	12.443	28.412	31.410	34.170	37.566	39.997	45.314
21	8.034	8.897	13.240	29.615	32.671	35.479	38.932	41.401	46.796
22	8.643	9.542	14.041	30.813	33.924	36.781	40.289	42.796	48.268
23	9.260	10.196	14.848	32.007	35.172	38.076	41.638	44.181	49.728
24	9.886	10.856	15.659	33.196	36.415	39.364	42.980	45.558	51.179
25	10.520	11.524	16.473	34.382	37.652	40.646	44.314	46.928	52.619
26	11.160	12.198	17.292	35.563	38.885	41.923	45.642	48.290	54.051
27	11.808	12.878	18.114	36.741	40.113	43.195	46.963	49.645	55.475
28	12.461	13.565	18.939	37.916	41.337	44.461	48.278	50.994	56.892
29	13.121	14.256	19.768	39.087	42.557	45.722	49.588	52.335	58.301
30	13.787	14.953	20.599	40.256	43.773	46.979	50.892	53.672	59.702
35	17.192	18.509	24.797	46.059	49.802	53.203	57.342	60.275	66.619
40	20.707	22.164	29.051	51.805	55.758	59.342	63.691	66.766	73.403

RANDOM NUMBERS

12	85	40	82	01	41	63	79	74	52	36	99	88	95	48	36	16	92	30	25
34	60	21	38	60	26	04	92	74	50	89	44	31	60	32	16	92	61	99	49
84	52	18	42	80	06	40	13	16	25	17	50	64	96	20	80	86	58	32	62
93	05	34	11	73	18	40	35	11	37	91	74	76	13	00	29	25	06	09	71
63	52	01	80	92	45	92	24	76	70	33	98	94	89	32	46	68	13	12	36
66	36	10	31	45	56	57	08	00	03	71	70	83	84	19	39	75	92	64	44
81	44	02	80	27	97	53	89	47	28	49	87	52	46	45	70	08	27	88	31
49	81	00	26	55	57	46	35	28	09	28	04	22	60	42	95	08	60	11	05
44	42	44	14	27	68	57	05	13	37	26	66	53	18	40	07	86	46	83	02
51	10	93	10	28	30	49	97	90	83	55	58	34	17	66	20	74	21	25	60
11	46	45	26	34	26	03	45	01	96	18	64	44	33	51	90	44	44	87	64
23	06	64	21	03	70	90	02	15	15	32	58	79	67	31	95	24	46	99	62
72	56	98	93	72	19	76	08	81	36	34	56	26	83	69	45	84	92	07	75
38	73	91	20	23	77	91	65	12	16	51	04	49	97	65	52	26	07	92	58
45	87	47	52	23	43	97	21	15	01	25	10	54	67	52	54	70	07	52	81
55	56	23	80	11	94	25	58	32	14	82	12	23	65	70	86	94	87	21	61
18	14	53	18	72	30	19	17	89	72	92	60	33	97	74	24	19	34	70	15
00	57	11	98	91	42	96	53	90	18	98	60	28	03	84	74	41	48	40	20
78	82	27	80	48	49	49	39	97	36	57	03	17	96	00	54	69	05	41	58
15	10	24	85	32	12	04	86	10	97	57	12	51	86	66	45	45	39	74	66
13	36	32	91	89	62	11	65	74	43	00	82	06	12	17	72	99	11	28	82
12	20	77	48	47	12	84	93	58	10	29	39	01	85	19	56	48	73	86	39
15	41	97	91	45	95	26	40	05	78	69	34	39	27	93	10	00	57	28	66
63	35	48	34	24	58	14	26	02	25	86	92	42	84	67	04	16	91	92	95
63	76	07	92	20	91	57	99	96	48	11	68	40	46	72	32	31	76	24	94
82	38	83	43	15	86	77	70	67	97	99	83	53	95	93	20	50	02	50	91
43	60	00	82	81	16	56	75	80	73	69	20	90	99	13	08	91	50	35	51
53	62	23	20	66	21	71	03	55	38	26	44	96	93	71	59	74	00	55	90
65	77	15	58	24	44	77	70	88	47	51	55	31	35	10	64	88	90	03	42
32	22	01	55	92	45	79	40	61	21	50	36	42	66	28	15	39	44	80	38
88	79	17	92	26	95	17	60	90	27	25	16	97	73	01	73	94	48	36	19
46	41	10	10	03	98	37	02	05	83	54	89	63	65	68	12	86	01	72	16

(continued)

Continued

12	93	20	18	02	48	17	76	89	45	41	57	48	19	22	00	05	83	87	52
39	69	29	38	80	48	15	13	30	80	22	31	40	25	68	30	44	67	66	86
34	26	06	45	46	12	63	44	70	22	12	70	34	12	15	03	15	37	50	70
36	33	21	88	57	38	06	99	87	56	50	17	49	11	70	08	09	57	77	35
48	43	62	41	63	12	50	13	95	88	57	38	58	60	93	83	79	86	18	91
85	01	42	75	32	20	88	07	97	96	70	21	01	76	90	17	65	55	61	03
95	54	15	04	88	07	48	06	11	03	24	04	67	41	56	43	96	30	53	35
00	33	65	58	72	61	68	76	88	92	79	49	27	95	01	63	99	68	49	53
97	06	25	63	21	57	42	24	38	87	02	90	33	10	28	46	88	74	58	44
38	98	93	21	89	19	20	14	30	84	36	51	32	64	11	01	88	98	42	14
87	80	11	29	93	56	52	85	93	16	82	83	85	07	42	47	37	01	84	23
24	25	15	18	36	37	19	44	88	60	03	52	68	00	08	92	47	23	97	96
46	95	83	45	40	70	72	47	60	02	02	96	33	00	16	13	70	38	02	35
80	37	03	89	19	56	01	10	18	03	69	46	32	95	50	00	28	95	25	83
87	37	59	61	25	79	39	08	68	33	80	67	12	60	27	38	07	30	06	98
39	97	55	52	41	93	06	61	46	80	66	06	34	80	18	28	72	41	06	77
56	96	90	80	95	47	70	53	41	69	73	88	15	91	19	50	61	43	66	30
21	25	33	25	68	64	01	99	66	64	26	09	71	53	27	35	06	33	50	56

BIBLIOGRAPHY

Anderson et al. (2007) *Statistics for Business and Economics*, London: Thomson.

Anderson et al. (2008) *An introduction to management science*, Twelfth edition, Mason, Ohio: Thomson.

Barboianu, C. (2006) *Probability Guide to Gambling: The Mathematics of Dice, Slots*. Roulette, Baccarat, Blackjack, Poker, Lottery and Sports Bets, Infarom. Craiova, Romania

Blastland, M. and Dilnot, A. (2007) *The tiger that isn't: Seeing through a world of numbers*, Croydon, UK: Profile Books.

Curwin, J. and Slater, R. (2008) *Quantitative Methods for Business Students*, sixth edition, London: Thomson.

Collis, J. and Hussey, R. (2009) *Business Research. A practical guide for under- graduate and postgraduate students*, Third edition, London: Palgrave Macmillan.

Eastaway, R. and Haigh, J. (2011) *The Hidden Mathematics of Sport: Beating the Odds in Your Favourite Sports*, London: Portico.

Fowler, F. (2013) *Survey Research Methods*, Fifth edition, London: Sage.

Haigh, J. (2000) *Taking Chances*, Oxford, UK: Oxford University Press.

Hammond, S. et al. (2012) 'Air traffic control, business regulation and CO2 emissions', *OR Insight*, 25, 3, 127–149.

Lumby, S. and Jones, C (1999) *Fundamentals of Investment Appraisal*, Kentucky USA: Cengage.

Makridakis et al. (1998) *Forecasting: Methods and Applications*, Third edition, London: Wiley.

McClave, J. and Sincich, T. (2006) *Statistics*, Tenth edition, Prentice Hall, New Jersey.

Morris, C. (2012) *Quantitative Approaches in Business Studies*, Eighth edition, London: Prentice Hall.

Oakshott, L. (2012) *Essential Quantitative Methods*, Fifth edition, London: Palgrave Macmillan.

Rienthonga, T. Walker, A. and Bektas, T. (2011) 'Look, here comes the library van! Optimizing the timetable of the mobile library service on the Isle of Wight', *OR Insight*, 24, 1, 49–62.

Rowe, N. (2002) *Refresher in Basic Mathematics*, 3rd edition, London: Thompson Learning.

Sheldon, R. (2010) *Introduction to Probability Models*, Tenth edition, Oxford, UK: Academic press.

Swift, L. and Piff, S. (2010) *Quantitative Methods*, Third edition, London: Palgrave Macmillan.

Tukey, J.W. (1991) *The Philosophy of Multiple Comparisons*, Statistical Science, 6, 100–116.

Vile, J.L. et al. (2012) 'Predicting ambulance demand using singular spectrum analysis', *Journal of the Operational Research Society*, 63, 1556–1565.

Wisniewski, M. *Quantitative Methods for Decision Makers*, Fifth edition, London: Prentice Hall.

Wright, M. (2009) '50 years of OR in sport', *Journal of the Operational Research Society*, 60, S161–S168.

INDEX